Lebanon

Lebanon

BY TERRI WILLIS

Enchantment of the World
Second Series

Children's Press®

A Division of Scholastic Inc.

NEW YORK TORONTO LONDON AUCKLAND SYDNEY
MEXICO CITY NEW DELHI HONG KONG
DANBURY, CONNECTICUT

Frontispiece: Sunset over medieval mosque in Beirut

Consultant: Amy J. Johnson, Assistant Professor of History, Berry College, Mount Berry, GA

Please note: All statistics are as up-to-date as possible at the time of publication.

Book production by Herman Adler Design

Library of Congress Cataloging-in-Publication Data

Willis, Terri.
  Lebanon / by Terri Willis. — 1st ed.
          p. cm. — (Enchantment of the world. Second series)
  Includes bibliographical references and index.
  ISBN 0-516-23685-7
  1. Lebanon—Juvenile literature. I. Title. II. Series.
      DS80.W.48 2004
      956.92—dc22   2004005174

Lebanon

Contents

Cover photo:
Crusader Castle
of Sidon

City of Tyre

Phoenician jars

Highs and Lows

I F YOU NEEDED TO SUM UP ALL OF LEBANON IN JUST A FEW short words, "highs and lows" might work. From its dramatic landscape and diverse climate to its lengthy history, Lebanon is a series of things that range from high to low.

Even though it is one of the world's smallest countries, Lebanon includes some dramatically different terrains. Its mountainous region reaches high to the sky, with some peaks reaching taller than 10,000 feet (3,048 meters). Yet not far from the mountains, the elevation drops quickly to sea level on the shores of the Mediterranean Sea.

Opposite: **The landscape of Lebanon varies from plains and valleys to coastal areas and mountains. This is a view of the mountains near Aagoura.**

Fishing boats on the Mediterranean coast

Geopolitical map of Lebanon

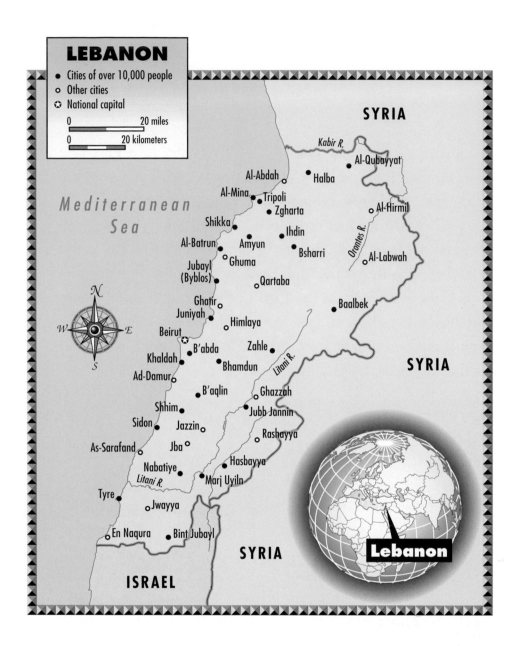

The climate, too, varies drastically. Lebanon is one of those rare places where you can sun on the beach in the morning, then take a short drive in the car and be skiing in the mountains in the afternoon. There are seasonal variations, of course, but generally temperatures along the coast are warm, while not far away, the mountains are cool and snowy much of the year.

Lebanon's history has its own series of highs and lows. In ancient times, it was a spectacular place, a center of trade, culture, and scientific innovation. But this greatness encouraged other countries to conquer and take control. Lebanon's people endured many centuries of lows, periods when they had to struggle and fight to regain their freedom and glory. Again and again this land and its people have been knocked down, only to get back up again and reclaim their position in the world. In 1943 the country finally became independent, and its reputation reached new heights. Many called Lebanon's capital city, Beirut, "the Paris of the Middle East." It earned the title for its great museums, glittering hotels and restaurants, and many successful businesses and banks.

During the mid-1970s until the early 1990s, however, Lebanon suffered a bitter and violent civil war. Many of the problems were rooted in the strong political differences of its citizens, which had grown worse over previous decades. Some 150,000 lives were

Bombing during the civil war in Lebanon severely damaged the U.S. Embassy in Beirut.

After war's end, Lebanon
began the process of growth
and recovery.

lost. Many of Lebanon's buildings were ruined, especially in Beirut. The country suffered severe environmental damage from bombings and neglect and misuse of the land. Finally, after years of attempts at peace, the war came to an end.

In recent years, the country has been rebuilding—not only its cities and its environment but its reputation as well. The arts in Lebanon are flourishing. Novelists, poets, and journalists are gaining importance as people turn to the written word, giving them a way to express their thoughts and feelings. Music, from traditional folk to modern rock, is stirring people's emotions.

Lebanon is once again becoming a tourist destination, the kind of place people are eager to visit for its natural beauty and culture. Lebanon has great seaside resorts and wonderful mountain lodges.

Opportunities for outdoor activities such as hiking, skiing, and bicycling abound. Lebanese people are also enjoying sports—both those they participate in, and those they watch. There are fine museums highlighting the country's lengthy history. The warmth of its people, so long hidden by the terror of war, is emerging too.

All signs point upward, to another high point in Lebanon's history.

Unique in the Middle East

L EBANON IS A SMALL NATION IN ASIA. IT IS A LONG, NAR-row expanse of land, bordered on the north and east by Syria and on the south by Israel. Its western border is the Mediterranean Sea.

A Middle Eastern Nation

Lebanon is one of the nations of the Middle East, the name given by Europeans to the region that lies between Europe and eastern Asia. People living there call it *al-sharq al-Awsat.* There is some disagreement about which countries make up the Middle East. Those most often identified as Middle Eastern countries are Lebanon, Bahrain, Egypt, Iran, Iraq, Israel, Jordan, Kuwait, Qatar, Oman, Saudi Arabia, Syria, Turkey, United Arab Emirates, and Yemen. Other countries sometimes listed as part of the Middle East include Libya, Tunisia, Algeria, Morocco, and Sudan.

About 290 million people live in the Middle East in an area that covers about 2.8 million square miles (7.25 million square kilometers.) Very little Middle Eastern land—only about 5 percent—can be used to grow crops. Most of the land is desert, along with scrub and mountains. The Middle East produces most of the world's oil, some 16 million barrels each day. Lebanon's geography, however, is very different from that of most other Middle Eastern countries.

Lebanon Is Unique

Lebanon is a lush, green country. Oil wells are not a feature of the country's landscape; in fact, no oil has been found in Lebanon. Instead there are snow-covered mountain peaks. Lebanese people do not suffer from dusty sandstorms that sting the eyes. Here, heavy mists that often settle into the mountain valleys make vision difficult.

There are four main geographic regions in Lebanon. They are not clearly defined by set borders, nor do they correspond to any political boundaries. There is the coastal plain, the Lebanon Mountains, the Anti-Lebanon Mountains, and the Bekaa Valley.

Unlike many Middle Eastern countries, Lebanon features growth and vegetation.

The Coastal Plain

The coastal plain is Lebanon's smallest region. It runs along the length of the country's shoreline with the Mediterranean Sea, some 135 miles (217 km). At its widest, it is only about 8 miles (13 km). Still, most of the country's population is located here. Beirut, Lebanon's capital and largest city, is located on the coast along with such other major cities as Tripoli, Byblos, Sidon, and Tyre.

The region has a long history going back to ancient times. Byblos is one of the world's oldest continually inhabited towns. People have lived here for more than seven thousand years, and it's easy to understand why. It contains a natural harbor that attracted sailors and fishermen, and good soil, where early farmers planted grains. It was, throughout much of history, a

Byblos

The Lebanese city of Byblos has had several names throughout its lengthy history. In the Bible it was referred to as Gubla; later it was known as Giblet or Jbail. The name Byblos, though, dates to time even before the Bible. It comes from *bublos*, which in Greek means "papyrus." This is a grasslike plant grown in northern Africa, with stems that were used for writing upon. In ancient times, papyrus was traded from Egypt to Greece, and Byblos was a major shipping port along the route. When many papyrus sheets were collected together, they were called a *biblion*, meaning "book." The Bible takes its name from this.

prosperous and orderly community, a religious center with a strong economy in trade. Today visitors come to enjoy the natural beauty of the coast and the historic charm of the city.

The Lebanon Mountains

The Lebanon Mountains give the nation its name and are Lebanon's most striking geographic feature. Approximately 100 miles (160 km) long, with a width of 6 to 35 miles (10 to 56 km), it's a large mountain range. It is bordered on the west by the country's coastal plain, with the Bekaa Valley to the east. Lebanese cedar trees, a famous symbol of the country, grow here, though they were once far more numerous than they are today.

The country's highest point, at an elevation of 10,131 feet (3,088 m), is Qurnet as Sawda. This peak is located just southeast of the coastal city of Tripoli. Farther south is the nation's second-highest peak, Jabal Sannin, at a height of 8,620 feet (2,627 m). As the range continues southward the peaks get lower and gradually become the Hills of Galilee. There are several popular ski resorts tucked among the slopes throughout this region. They lure thousands of people out of Lebanon's cities on the weekends to ski and relax.

The Lebanese Mountains

The Rivers of Lebanon

During the rainy winter season Lebanon has many rivers. Most are temporary, though, caused by melting snow and rain running off the western slopes of the Lebanon Mountains.

There are only three rivers that flow year-round. The Kabir River in the north creates the boundary between Lebanon and Syria. The Orontes River has its headwaters in a large basin in the Bekaa Valley, where it irrigates the soil. Known locally as Nahr al-Aasi in Arabic, it flows northward to Syria and is a popular river for kayaking trips. The ancient Romans built their city Baalbek near the headwaters of Lebanon's Litani River (above), or Nahr Litani. During its course of more than 90 miles (145 km) the Litani also irrigates the Bekaa Valley on its southward journey to the Mediterranean Sea.

One of the more important seasonal rivers is the Nahr al-Kalb, or Dog River (below), which drains into the Mediterranean just north of Beirut. It was once known as the Lycus River but was renamed for a statue of a wolf located near the river crossing. The steep slopes of the river gorge made it difficult for armies to cross. Those armies that made it across successfully often left a plaque or a medallion on the hillside as a thanksgiving. Today a bridge spans the river, so armies no longer face danger, but the tradition continues. Some Christian militias left memorials on the riverbank during the recent civil war.

The Anti-Lebanon Mountains

The Anti-Lebanon Mountains and the Hermon Mountains rise along Lebanon's eastern border with Syria. They are two separate mountain ranges, although they are often thought of as one. Though they generally have lower elevations than the Lebanon Mountains, they do rise in the north. Mount Hermon is the region's highest peak at 9,232 feet (2,814 m). There are few cities in these mountains, as they are too rugged for people to settle in.

Adonis and His Valley

The Adonis Valley was cut through Lebanon's mountains by the seasonal Nahr Ibrahim, or Ibrahim River, as it flowed to the sea. This beautiful valley is marked by rugged scenery and several ancient ruins.

Both the valley and the river take their name from the Greek god Adonis. The mythology surrounding him had its beginnings with the ancient Phoenicians who lived in the region that is now Lebanon. According to mythology, Adonis was a beautiful baby who grew up to become a shepherd. He and the goddess Aphrodite fell in love and shared their first kiss in this valley. But at a young age Adonis was killed by a wild boar while hunting along the river that today bears his name. The river water, which turns red each spring, was believed to be the blood of Adonis. Actually the red coloring comes from minerals in the soil.

Lebanon's Geographical Features

Area: 4,015 square miles (10,399 sq km)

Greatest Distance North to South: 120 miles (193 km)

Greatest Distance East to West: 50 miles (80 km)

Land and Water Borders: Syria to the north and west, Israel to the south, and the Mediterranean Sea to the west

Highest Elevation: 10,131 feet (3,088 m) at Qurnet as Sawda

Lowest Elevation: sea level, at the coast of the Mediterranean Sea

Length of Coastline: 135 miles (217 km)

Highest Average Temperature: 90°F (32°C)

Lowest Average Temperature: 55°F (13°C)

Average Annual Precipitation: coast, 35 inches (89 cm); mountains, up to 50 inches (127 cm)

The Bekaa Valley

The Bekaa Valley is bordered by the Lebanon Mountains to the west and the Anti-Lebanon Mountains to the east. This is a fertile region that stops at the Jordan Valley in the south and stretches approximately 100 miles (160 km) northward into

the plains of Syria. Its width varies from 5 to 10 miles (8 to 16 km). The Bekaa Valley is part of a chain of valleys, running from the Middle East south through Africa to Mozambique, called the Great East African Rift System. It's the largest portion of level land in Lebanon, but it becomes hilly at its southern end.

The Bekaa Valley has some of the Middle East's most fertile farmland, containing soil rich with nutrients and clay that wash down from the surrounding mountains. This farmland has long supplied grain to people throughout the world. In ancient times Roman conquerors shipped out wheat grown in the valley to their capital in Italy. Other foreign invaders throughout the centuries also helped themselves to the produce grown in the Bekaa. Today the Bekaa Valley provides most of the food for the nation.

Among the major cities in the Bekaa Valley are Chtaura, Zahle, and Baalbek. Chtaura is the region's center for banking, trade, and transport, as well as a location for frequent political conferences between officials from Lebanon and from its important neighbor Syria. Zahle, meanwhile, is more of a tourist destination. The Birdawni River flows right through this attractive resort city.

Baalbek is known for its ancient ruins. Many consider it to be one of the most important Roman sites in the Middle East. There are remains of several spectacular temples. One of them, the Temple of Jupiter, was built during the first

Baalbek is a fine example of Roman architecture.

century A.D. and was the largest of all Roman temples in ancient times. Only six of its massive columns still stand. At 66 feet (20 m) tall, they are a hint of the majesty that once was.

Climate

Lebanon has a Mediterranean climate. Summers are long and hot, with highs in July and August that regularly reach 90 degrees Fahrenheit (32 degrees Celsius). The country's warmest temperatures most often occur along the coastal plain. The mountains are cooler, and the pleasant, fresh air provides a welcome escape for urban vacationers.

Lebanon's winters, from December through March, are short and fairly warm. Lows in January and February rarely sink below 55°F (13°C), except in the higher mountain elevations where temperatures can dip below freezing. This is the peak wet season, especially along the coast and in nearby mountains. Most of the country's seventy to eighty-five rainy days each year occur in winter. Warm winds blowing across the Mediterranean pick up moisture, then dump it as rain once the air cools as it blows over the cooler land. The coastal plain typically receives 30 to 45 inches (76 to 114 centimeters) of rainfall each year, with up to 50 inches (127 cm) each year in the Lebanon Mountains and a bit less in the Anti-Lebanon Mountains. The country's main agricultural area, the Bekaa Valley, is so sheltered between the two mountain ranges that it receives very little rainfall. It gets most of its moisture from the runoff coming down from surrounding slopes. Strong winds blow through the valley between the mountains.

Looking at Lebanon's Cities

Tripoli, with a population of 212,900, is Lebanon's second-largest city. Though it's a modern coastal city, it has held on to much of its history. People have lived here since the fourteenth century B.C. Tripoli has centuries-old mosques and churches. It has *souqs* (above)—outdoor markets—and public baths built more than five hundred years ago. The city was famous for soap-making during the eighteenth century. Soaps made with honey and olive oil, in various shapes and scents, were in demand throughout Europe. Today Tripoli is a center for banking and trade.

People have lived in Sidon since about 6,000 B.C.

Today it has a population of 149,000. It suffered heavy damage during Lebanon's civil war and is working on rebuilding its economy and tourist industry. Like many of Lebanon's other ancient cities, Sidon contains ruins of historic buildings. One of the most unusual is the Sea Castle, built in the thirteenth century. Located 262 feet (80 m) offshore, it was originally the site of a Phoenician temple and later become a fortified structure to protect Crusaders from invaders. There was once a wooden footbridge that could be removed to keep out enemies, but visitors today can reach it by a permanent walkway. Tourists in Sidon also enjoy its beaches.

Tyre (below) is home to about 117,100 residents. It was established around 3000 B.C. as a small shore community along with a small island settlement. When King Hiram of Tyre had the two joined by a landfill two thousand years later, Tyre began to grow in size and importance. A center for shipping and trade, it was so influential that the Mediterranean Sea became known as the Tyrian Sea. There are several archaeological sites here, including a Roman hippodrome. This stadium, with seating for twenty thousand, was used for dangerous chariot races. Today people jog there. Other popular activities are fishing in Tyre's attractive harbor, shopping in its souqs, and relaxing at the beach.

Cedar Trees and Much More

LEBANON IS FAMOUS FOR ITS CEDARS: BEAUTIFUL, MAJESTIC trees that have played an important role in the history of the country. But though the cedars are the centerpiece of the nation's plant and animal life, there is much more. The country has great geographic diversity—warm coastlines and chilly mountains, thick forests and grassy plains. These differing habitats support a variety of plants and animals.

Opposite: **Al-Shouf Cedar Reserve in northern Lebanon**

Thick forests cover the Lebanese Mountains.

Lebanon's Plants

Forests, most notably the cedar trees that grew along the hilly coast, once covered much of Lebanon. But for five thousand years, the trees have been cut to build boats, palaces, homes, and more. More land has been cleared by fires and churned by plows. The civil war destroyed even more of the forests. It's now rare to see young cedar trees growing in the wild. Still, Lebanon is considered to be the most densely forested country in the Middle East.

Lebanese Cedar Trees

A Lebanese cedar tree is the symbol that adorns the Lebanese flag, for good reason. Even before biblical times, the country was known for its cedar trees. Extensive forests once covered Lebanon's hills, watered by moisture from evaporation over the Mediterranean. Thousands of years ago men cut the trees and carried them to the sea, where they were floated to other locations throughout the region. The lumber was highly prized and a symbol of wealth and power. Palaces, temples, and magnificent homes were constructed using Lebanese cedar.

Lebanese cedar trees provided the richly carved paneling for the Temple of Solomon, an important structure in the Old Testament, which was built by Lebanese workers. The illustration (right) depicts workmen moving felled trees to be used in the building

of the Temple of Solomon. The great tombs of the pharaohs of Egypt hold Lebanese cedar.

Wildflowers grow in abundance in the Lebanese Mountains.

Several types of pine trees grow in Lebanon's mountains, as well as oak, juniper, cypress, beech, cherry, and apple trees. Most of these low-growing trees are found in the middle elevations of the country as well. There the air is scented with such fragrant shrubs as sage, oleander, myrtle, and lavender. Lebanon violets and other wildflowers lend color and beauty.

In the lower elevations most of the trees and shrubs are cultivated for human use. These include such fruit trees as banana, orange, lemon, and olive. There are also medlar trees. Medlars are a fruit similar to crab apples that are best eaten when nearly rotten. Grains, too, are grown in the lower elevations along with many types of vegetables. Also grown there are grapes used to produce Lebanon's famous wines.

A ripe medlar

Lebanon's Animals

Just as many of Lebanon's trees were lost when their environment was destroyed, so too has the country lost many of its large mammals. Pollution and hunting have nearly wiped out several species of bears, gazelles, ibex, wild boars, and wolves, among other animals. Efforts are under way to keep these animals alive on nature reserves.

Lebanon makes great efforts to protect its wildlife. Animals such as the ibex are protected on nature reserves.

The jackal is at home in Lebanon.

Smaller mammals fare better than larger ones in situations with damaged habitats, since their needs aren't as great. It's easier for them to find the resources they need even on a smaller piece of land. Squirrels, foxes, wildcats, hares, badgers, hedgehogs, hyenas, jackals, porcupines, and martens are among the smaller mammals found in Lebanon. Lebanon's reptiles include geckos, snakes, and chameleons.

Lebanon's Ancient Spiderweb

Large dinosaurs roamed the earth more than 100 million years ago, and so did spiders. The oldest spider silk in existence, dating back 130 million years, was found in Lebanon. The silky bit of web had been trapped in a glob of sap that oozed from a tree. Over time the sap hardened into a chunk of amber. A Swiss researcher discovered it just a few years ago. Until this one was found, the oldest known spider silk was 30 million years old.

Amber, in which the silk is encapsulated, is fossilized tree resin. It hardens into a transparent, usually colored, chunk. Small insects or pieces of plant material are often trapped inside the resin (right), and they remain in the amber as preserved pieces of ancient history.

Amber has for centuries been popular in the Middle East. Men carried polished pieces of it as worry beads, and craftsmen used it to make amulets and other decorative items. But the amber used was usually imported from Europe. Lebanon's amber wasn't discovered until 1875. The first amber found there was a pretty, deep red color, but since it didn't contain any plant or insect particles, it was of little scientific value. Later collections taken from the Bekaa Valley turned up amber rich in fossils. These fossils enable scientists to study things preserved from millions of years ago.

Scientists studying the very old spiderweb have determined that it was most likely spun by an ancestor of the modern comb-footed spider. This is the only type of spider that spins this type of silky web near tree trunks, where it is most likely to get stuck in sap.

Life in the Air and the Water

Birds are plentiful in Lebanon. The coast is an important resting spot for migratory birds as they fly between Africa and Europe. More than 170 types of migratory birds have been spotted along the coast. The Palm Islands Reserve, off the coast of Al-Mina, is even more popular. Some three hundred bird species stop by while migrating, and several types of nonmigratory birds make these islands their home. Terns, broad-billed sandpipers, finches, ospreys, and mistle thrushes nest on the Palm Islands year-round. Other birds that live on both the islands and the coast include ducks, herons, flamingos, and pelicans.

Herons are among Lebanon's coastal birds.

As they rest during migration, hoopoes can be found in Lebanon.

Millions of birds also make the Bekaa Valley a resting point during their lengthy flights. Among the birds seen there are golden eagles, storks, buzzards, red-rumped swallows, kingfishers, cuckoos, kestrels, woodpeckers, and hoopoes. In the country's mountainous regions, birds include imperial eagles, Scop's owls, falcons, red kites, Bonelli's eagles, Sardinian warblers, hawks, and buzzards.

The waters off the coast are filled with fish and other marine life. Mediterranean turtles and green sea turtles, both rare species, live near the Palm Islands, along with Mediterranean monk seals.

The civil war was harmful to Lebanon's environment.

Environmental Damage

In Lebanon's agricultural regions, farming practices have destroyed much of the wilderness. Trees have been cut or burned down to prepare land for planting. Cattle overgraze on the grassy plains, depleting the land and the soil. Overuse of fertilizers and pesticides causes pollution, as do factories and waste from urban areas. The land and water around the large city of Beirut are especially vulnerable to this type of damage.

The many years of civil war hurt the environment as well. The most obvious destruction came from bombs. Buildings and neighborhoods were ruined, trees were downed, and the land was scarred with craters and rubble. The damage was massive.

Gas and electric services were interrupted during the war. As a result, people cut down and burned trees to provide heat and a means for cooking. The loss of trees made it easier for wind and rain to carry away the topsoil, the part of the earth that holds the most nutrients. This type of damage—erosion—makes it much more difficult for things to grow.

During the fighting, other services were cut off, too. Garbage wasn't collected regularly, and wastewater wasn't always tested. Pollutants were dumped into the sea. Rubbish was allowed to pile up and it, too, ended up in the Mediterranean. Much of Lebanon's toxic waste was dumped into the sea, as well as toxic waste from other countries that had paid Lebanon to dispose of their waste. Some of this has since been cleaned up, and much of the waste is now in landfill sites. There are still polluted areas along Lebanon's coasts, however, and trash is still sometimes seen in valleys and ditches.

Lebanon's coast still suffers from pollution.

While the government was preoccupied with the war, there was little control over construction. Unplanned building occurred in environmentally sensitive areas, especially along the coast and on hillsides. Logging and mining took place in areas where it was illegal but overlooked.

Undoing the Damage

The country is not letting these problems continue, though. The Lebanese government established a ministry of the environment in 1993. It helps manage the nation's environmental affairs by protecting natural, forestry, and archeological sites. It ensures clean drinking water, prevents sewage from causing marine pollution, and regulates urban development, hunting, fishing, and toxic-waste disposal.

The ministry of the environment also manages nature reserves. These are areas where as many of the factors that can damage the environment are eliminated as possible. The three Palm Islands and the Horsh Ehden mountain area were declared nature reserves in 1992, and in 1996 the al-Shouf Cedar Reserve was established.

Though these nature reserves are relatively new, the concept of preserving parts of the environment has been a part of Lebanese planning for generations. In the second century, the Roman emperor Hadrian preserved some of Lebanon's forests. He used inscriptions on rocks to mark protected areas where such trees as firs, junipers, cypresses, and, of course, cedars were not to be cut down.

Lebanon's Nature Reserves

The Palm Islands Reserve consists of three islands: Palm, Sanani, and Ramkine. The protected area is about 2 square miles (5 sq km) of land, some 3 miles (5 km) off the coast of Al-Mina. This eastern Mediterranean marine ecosystem is important for a number of reasons. It provides a resting spot

for thousands of migratory birds. It's also a place for the threat-ened Mediterranean turtles, loggerhead turtles, and green sea turtles to lay their eggs.

Newly hatched green sea turtles make their way to water's edge.

The Palm Islands reserve is a popular place for residents of Lebanon's crowded cities to escape to for fresh air and relax-ation. There they can hike on paths through the natural areas and sunbathe or swim at the beaches.

Horsh Ehden Nature Reserve, sometimes called the Forests of Ehden, covers about 6.5 square miles (17 sq km). Located just 2 miles (3 km) from the city of Ehden, it is within the northern Lebanon Mountains. Elevations in the reserve range from about 4,275 feet (1,300 m) to 6,410 feet (1,950 m).

Horsh Ehden is a refuge for several of Lebanon's endangered and rare mammals. Among these are species of weasels, badgers, squirrels, and martens. Wolves and hyenas are found here too. Migratory birds stop in Horsh Ehden to rest along their journey.

It's only a small part of Lebanon's land, covering less than 1 percent of the nation's total. However, some 40 percent of the country's plant types—more than one thousand species—have been recorded here. There are five hundred types of flowering plants and thirty-nine species of trees. The highlight of the reserve's plant life, however, is the large stand of native cedar.

Cedar is also the centerpiece of al-Shouf Cedar Reserve. It is Lebanon's largest nature reserve; at 212 square miles (549 sq km) it covers about 5 percent of the country's land. Three of the six cedar forests here contain old-growth cedars, some estimated to be two thousand years old.

Al-Shouf contains some one hundred types of birds along with numerous species of mammals, including wolves and gazelles. There is also a great diversity of plant life including many trees, shrubs, and grasses. Visitors can hike and snowshoe through the reserve in winter and mountain-bike in summer.

These three nature reserves hold Lebanon's best hopes for the protection of its environmental riches.

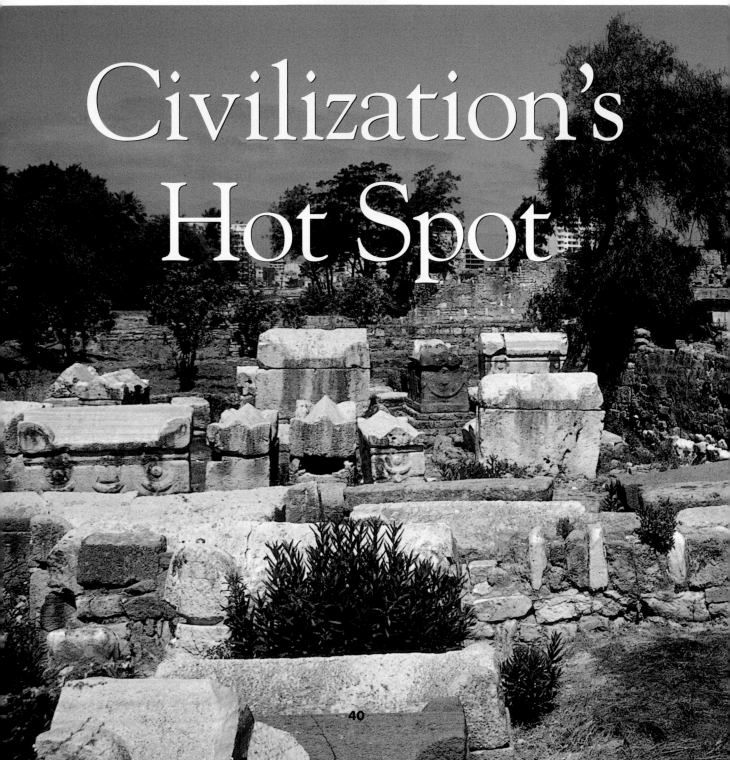

Civilization's Hot Spot

L EBANON HAS BEEN AN INDEPENDENT COUNTRY FOR ONLY a little more than a half-century. It nonetheless has a rich history, one that stretches across the span of human time. For centuries Lebanon was a hot spot of civilization, spreading culture and religion to people throughout the world.

Lebanon's Geography

Lebanon's location and geography are important parts of the story of its past. Streams that pour down from the mountains to the coast cut deep gorges into the landscape. These gorges made it difficult for large groups of people to move up and down the coast, while steep mountains and dense forests prevented easy travel inland. The ancient people who arrived on Lebanon's shores beginning around 10,000 B.C. settled near the water. Relatives of Canaanites, they had come from the Arabian Peninsula. They gathered in areas with safe natural harbors, large plains, and fertile land.

By around 3000 B.C. their settlements had evolved into a group of coastal cities known as Phoenicia. This name came from the Greeks, who called the residents Phoenicians because they traded a purple dye, *phoinikies*, made from murex shells. Though they shared a name and

Phoenicians settled along the coasts of Lebanon and traded goods among each other.

communicated and traded with each other, the Phoenician cities never unified politically. Instead each conducted business on it own and became known for its distinct characteristics and practices of its residents.

The cities that became known as centers of religion and trade were Berytus, which is now Beirut, and Gubla, which became Byblos. Gubla's residents sent olive oil, wine, and cedar to Egyptian pharaohs, getting gold, ivory, and metals in return. Trade in products such as weapons, glass, and dyes was an important activity for the cities of Tyre and Sidon as well. Both cities were also known for their residents' great abilities as sailors. Another of Phoenicia's major cities was settled by people who had come from Tyre, Sidon, and the Phoenician city Arwad. Each group maintained its own separate area, walled off from the others. The name of this city become Tripoli, which means "three cities."

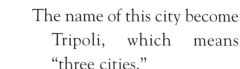

A Successful Society

The Phoenicians had become very successful by about 1100 B.C. They had developed their own alphabet, which enabled them to greatly improve communications. Their goods, such as carved ivory, textiles,

Phoenician goods such as these glass jars were highly desired objects.

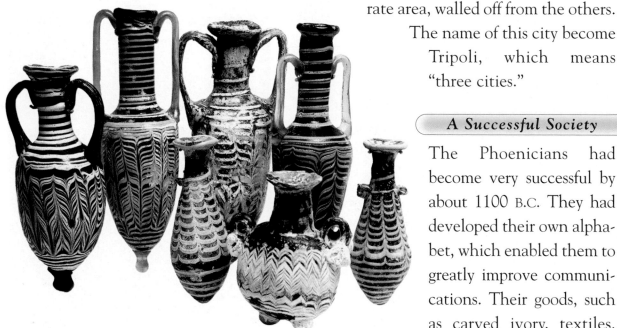

beautiful glass, and metal, were prized throughout western Asia and Europe. They were accomplished shipbuilders and navigators who controlled the Mediterranean Sea for nearly five centuries.

The Fall of Phoenicia

While the Phoenicians were excellent traders, they were not skilled soldiers. This became their downfall. Their stronghold on Mediterranean trade came to an end in 867 B.C., when the

The Phoenician Alphabet

Our modern alphabet owes a great deal to the Phoenicians, who are credited with developing the first alphabet. The earliest known example of the Phoenician alphabet dates back to the eleventh century B.C. It was an inscription on the sarcophagus of King Hiram in Byblos. Prior to the development of the Phoenician alphabet, only specially trained scribes were able to record language, using complex symbols and hieroglyphics. When the Phoenician alphabet was developed, with only twenty-two symbols, communication became far less complicated. This helped trade flourish and contributed to the success of the Phoenicians.

The word *phonics* comes from *Phoenician* and the Phoenicians' revolutionary idea of using simple symbols to represent the sounds of language.

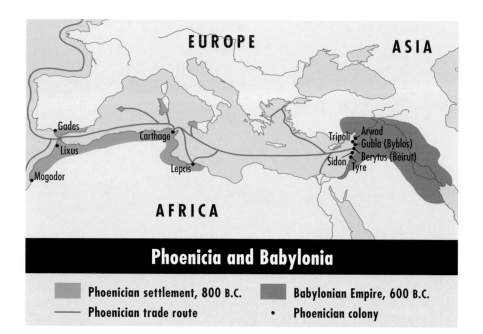

EUROPE   ASIA

Gades

Lixus

Mogodor

Carthage

Lepcis

AFRICA

Tripoli
Arwad
Gubla (Byblos)
Berytus (Beirut)
Sidon
Tyre

Phoenicia and Babylonia

Phoenician settlement, 800 B.C.   Babylonian Empire, 600 B.C.

Phoenician trade route   • Phoenician colony

The Persian army conquered Lebanon in 538 B.C. However, the Phoenicians welcomed them as they were released from the Babylonian stronghold.

Assyrians became the first group of outsiders to conquer the Phoenicians and their homeland, which they called Lebanon. Next came the Babylonians in 590 B.C. Another fifty-two years later, in 538 B.C., Persians took over Lebanon. The Phoenicians saw them as liberators, freeing them from the Babylonians.

Throughout this era of invasions, the Phoenicians managed to maintain some degree of independence and were able to keep their identity. But when the Greeks, led by Alexander the Great, conquered much of the Middle East during the fourth century B.C., Phoenician society began to blend in with that of the conquerors. Greece at that time was the leader of civilization and learning, and its

Greek and Roman Empires

Alexander's Empire, 323 B.C.	Roman Empire, early 2nd century
—— Modern-day Lebanon	

culture influenced much of Phoenician society. Greek society began to falter, though, after being pressured by a series of invaders.

Alexander the Great and his army conquered land throughout the Middle East.

In A.D. 64, a strong Roman army took over and brought the Phoenicians under their control. Eventually Lebanon became part of the Eastern Roman Empire, also known as the Byzantine Empire. Around A.D. 340, the Roman Empire started to lose some of its power when the Goths began their invasion of Europe. As the Romans were distracted, fending off their enemies, their power began to crumble, too. The empire came undone.

Christianity

Saints Peter and Paul both traveled to Lebanon spreading Christianity.

While the Roman Empire was failing, a new religion was growing throughout the region, replacing several ancient religions that worshipped many gods. Christianity was becoming a major force. This faith was established by the followers of Jesus Christ in the beginning of the first century A.D. One of Jesus' followers, Saint Paul, had spent some time in Lebanon spreading the faith. Another follower, Saint Peter, did even more to spread Jesus' message about God, forgiveness, and eternal life in heaven. This was an attractive message to many, and people throughout the region began to turn to Christianity.

At the same time, though, Christianity's growing popularity made many people angry. Some felt that Christianity had been forced on them by the Byzantine Empire. People in authority felt threatened by the way Christians obeyed the rules of their faith more strictly than the laws of the land. People who followed other religions feared that their own religious freedom might be taken away. Christians themselves were caught in struggles over differences in their beliefs and divided into several sects that fought among themselves. Many Christians were tortured and killed.

Lebanon's mountains had been nearly impossible for invading armies to cross, and now the mountains offered a safe haven to those who feared being persecuted because of their faith. One of the sects that fled to the mountains for safety were the Maronites, a large Christian group based in Lebanon.

The Spread of Islam

Islam began to spread across the Middle East shortly after the year 630, bringing changes to the region's culture and politics. In 636 the religion took hold in Lebanon. The first great Muslim dynasty was the Umayyads, who

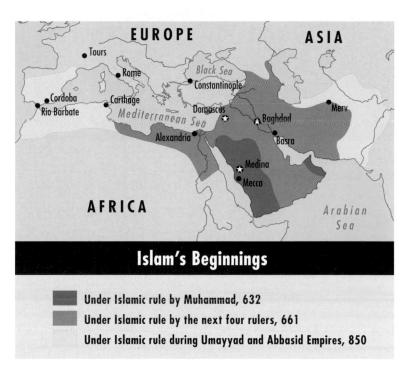

Islam's Beginnings

Under Islamic rule by Muhammad, 632

Under Islamic rule by the next four rulers, 661

Under Islamic rule during Umayyad and Abbasid Empires, 850

Crusaders invaded Lebanon to rid the area of Muslims.

influenced Lebanon for about one hundred years. They didn't have unanimous support in the region, though, as Christians and Jews opposed their reign. The Umayyads were followed by the Abbasid Empire, which ruled until 1258.

During this period, Islam itself was undergoing changes. It divided into two major groups, Sunni Muslims and Shi'ite Muslims, over differences in leadership. Like the Christians before them, some of these Muslims found safety in the hills of Lebanon when they were persecuted for their faith. The Shi'ites took refuge there during the eleventh and twelfth centuries. Another sect, the Druze, hid in the mountains during the eleventh century.

The mountains weren't safe during the Crusades, however. In 1095, Christian leader Pope Urban II declared that the Holy Land should no longer be in the hands of Muslims. During this period Christian invaders from Europe, called the Crusaders, occupied much of the territory in Lebanon, mountains included. From 1095 to 1291, many Lebanese Christians, especially Maronites, fought alongside the Crusaders against Muslims and their authority. Additionally, some Christians took the side of Muslims, and some Muslims fought with the Crusaders. Thousands on both sides were killed, and several major cities were destroyed.

Late in the thirteenth century the Crusades came to an end when the Mamlukes of Egypt forced the Crusaders out of Lebanon and the rest of the region. After the Crusaders left, the Muslims and the Christians in Lebanon managed to tolerate each other. Each group had a lot of control over its own affairs and mostly lived independently of the other. The Maronites and the Druze lived in separate areas of the mountains, while the Shi'ites lived in southern and eastern Lebanon, and the Sunnis resided on the coast. During this period of relative peace, Lebanon's cities once again revived their trading practices and prospered.

The Ottoman military had strength in numbers and conquered much of the Middle East, including Lebanon.

The Ottomans Enter

Around the time the Crusades were ending, a new force was taking root. The Ottoman Empire had its early beginnings around 1300, when a group of nomadic Turks started gaining in numbers and strength. Within 150 years, this army had grown into a powerful force that controlled much

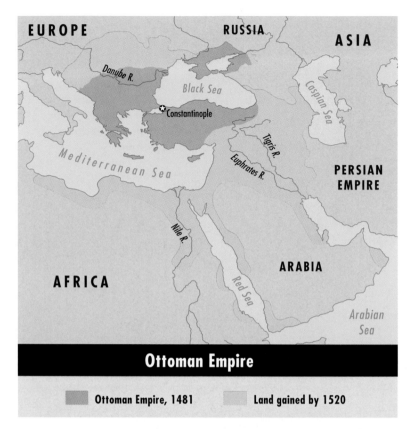

Ottoman Empire

Ottoman Empire, 1481	Land gained by 1520

of the Middle East. In 1516 the Ottomans added Lebanon to the regions they controlled and took over Egypt soon after. The Ottoman Empire was in place.

The Lebanese people, tired of bloodshed, did not revolt against their new Ottoman rulers. Left alone for the most part, they continued to prosper. New agricultural practices improved food production, and additions to ports increased trade. By the 1840s, Beirut had become

Fakhr al-Din M'an, Father of Modern Lebanon

Often called the Father of Modern Lebanon, Fakhr al-Din M'an accomplished several feats to earn that title. Born into the Druze faith, he was made a prince in 1590 by the Ottomans, who wanted better relations with the Druze. He took control of Beirut and was eventually able to include other lands and coastal cities under one rule for the first time. He was able to get the members of the Maronite faith to cooperate with the members of the Druze, even though the groups had been fighting.

With the region united and working together, Fakhr al-Din M'an was able to use his solid business sense to improve the economy. Beirut began trading with the Venetians and the rest of Europe. He modernized Lebanon's silk and olive-oil production, boosting business in those industries. Ports in Sidon and Beirut improved under his guidance, too.

By 1631 he was controlling even more land, including what is now Israel and Jordan. The Ottomans, angry with his power, decided to attack. Fakhr al-Din M'an fled into a cave outside Sidon. He was captured and brought to Istanbul, where he was executed in 1635. But many of the changes he brought to Lebanon remain in place today.

Trade flourished in Lebanon with Beirut as its major port.

the major port for trade in all of the Middle East. Ships traveled regularly to and from France, England, Greece, and Italy.

Religious Divisions

By 1842 the divisions between Lebanon's religious sects were again causing problems. This time European nations became involved and took sides. France supported Maronite Christians, while England supported the Druze in the bloody conflicts. In an effort to stop the fighting, the Ottoman government put a new idea into place. Lebanon would be divided in two, along a highway that ran from Beirut east into Damascus, Syria. To the north, Christians would govern. To the south, the Druze would be in charge.

Almost from its start, the division was a disaster. The north was not populated only by Christians, and the south was not just Druze territory. People of both faiths lived on both sides of the dividing line. Each group was distraught about having members of the other faith in power. Again violent fighting began.

Before long much of the country was in shambles. Sixty villages were destroyed. Armies from England, Austria, France, Prussia, and Russia got involved as the death toll climbed to more than ten thousand. An Ottoman foreign minister arrived in 1860 to try to stop the bloodshed. Through a series of treaties signed between 1861 and 1867 by the foreign countries involved, the fighting came to an end. The outsiders insisted that the Ottomans establish strict regulations to stop the conflicts. A national police force was put in place, and citizens received new rights, including the freedom to elect local leaders.

Though religious differences were still apparent, Lebanon once again began to flourish. Many Lebanese Christians traveled to Rome to study and brought back home with them Western ideas about culture and dress, which they joined with their native ideals. European missionaries came to Lebanon, establishing church-run schools. Universities opened, and hospitals offered quality care. Newspapers and books were popular and helped to spread information rapidly. Influences also came from Mediterranean, African, and Asian cultures. By 1915, Lebanon, and Beirut in particular, had taken on a very international flair.

French Control

But the glory came to an end with World War I. Germany was defeated in the war, and this brought with it the downfall of

the Ottoman Empire, which had allied itself with Germany. The Ottomans were forced to give up all its territories, including Lebanon. The League of Nations, an international organization similar to the United Nations, decided in 1920 that the regions that make up present-day Lebanon would be awarded to France as a mandate, a territory under its rule.

Several important changes took place in Lebanon during this period of French control. A Lebanese constitution was approved in 1926, and the country's name become the Republic of Lebanon. A Lebanese flag, with the cedar tree as

The League of Nations promoted international cooperation and peace.

its national symbol, was created. Beirut was named the capital city. Several government agencies were created to address the people's needs for education, safety, health care, and legislation. Citizens were guaranteed the freedom to observe the religion of their choice. However, local leaders were allowed no say in the government. France enforced its control through a strong military presence.

The most important change, one with long-lasting implications, was the creation of an unwritten agreement, the National Pact, which lives on today. It is a specific division of power between Christianity and Islam, called confessionalism, or a confessional democracy. It is unique throughout the world.

Lebanon's Confessional Democracy

Lebanon's leadership positions are filled by members of specific religions, based on census data about the proportion of Lebanese who practice those religions. This method, called confessionalism, became the rule in 1943 in the National Pact. At that time the most recent census was from 1932, when the majority of Lebanese were Maronite Christians, followed by Sunni Muslims and Shi'ite Muslims. So it was determined that the president of Lebanon was to be a Maronite Christian, the prime minister a Sunni Muslim, and the speaker of the National Assembly a Shi'ite Muslim. Positions in the National Assembly were allotted on a six-to-five ratio of Christians to Muslims. Other key government posts were also filled based on religious background. Even today, few people can get jobs anywhere within the Lebanese government if they don't belong to one of these major religions.

This system seemed reasonably fair in 1943, when the seats of power truly reflected the population. In the years since, however, the population of Lebanon has changed quite dramatically. Civil wars and refugee situations within Lebanon and its surrounding nations have caused thousands of people to move in or out. There are far more Muslims living in Lebanon today than there are Christians. Nonetheless, the Christians in charge of the government have held on to their power. There has not been an official census taken in Lebanon since 1932. Government leadership won't allow it. That means the Maronite Christians still hold the most important positions of power, even though they are no longer the majority.

When World War II broke out by 1939, France grabbed a stronger hold on Lebanon. It suspended the Lebanese constitution and took command of the Lebanese military. But the Lebanese people refused to give up their freedoms and put up great resistance to the changes. France soon gave in and in 1941 declared Lebanon to be a "sovereign and independent nation." Almost immediately, the United States and Great Britain stated their recognition of Lebanon as a new nation, and Lebanon acted quickly to remove any reference to France and French control from the Lebanese constitution.

This angered the French, who again tried to crack down on Lebanese freedoms. Riots broke out in Lebanon in protest, and many outside countries joined in support of Lebanese independence. France gave in. On November 22, 1943, Lebanon gained complete independence.

Refugees from Palestine found shelter in one of Lebanon's largest camps, The City That Hearts Built, in 1955.

Challenges abounded. There were problems with neighboring Israel during the 1948 Arab-Israeli War. Lebanon allowed people fleeing Israel to find safety within its borders. Most of these were Muslims who were left homeless when Jewish troops forced them out of Palestine. More people entered Lebanon in 1956,

Riots and looting took place in 1958 in Beirut in response to President Chamoun's policies.

when the Suez Canal War forced Arabs, Americans, and Europeans out of Israel and Egypt. In 1958, Lebanon faced further challenges. At a time when many Arab nations were emphasizing their common goals, President Camille Chamoun stressed Lebanon's commitment to the West. He was also trying to engineer a second term as president, something that would have required legal changes to the political system and that the Muslim population especially opposed. Revolts broke out in several cities, and Lebanon requested assistance from the United States to put down the rebellions.

Through it all, there was a great demand for housing and real estate. Banks were booming, and by 1963, Beirut was an international finance capital. This success, however, did not ensure any kind of peace. Throughout Lebanon's early years of independence, Muslims and Christians engaged in clashes over power.

Struggles Continue

The turmoil within the entire region only added to Lebanon's woes. The Six-Day War, fought in 1967, was just one of many battles. It occurred when the navies of several Arab nations that had been struggling against Israel joined forces to block Israel's access to international waterways. Israel struck back by bombing airfields owned by one of the nations, Egypt. Other Arab nations, Jordan and Syria, then attacked Israel. Israel responded by claiming a large chunk of land from both of these nations.

The war was over in a few days, but it sent Palestinian refugees from Jordan fleeing into Lebanon. Lebanon managed to remain out of the conflict until 1968, when Arab terrorists who claimed to be from a Palestinian refugee camp in Lebanon attacked an Israeli airplane. To retaliate, Israel bombed the airport in Beirut. Israel

In Egypt, Israeli soldiers drive their vehicles in a convoy during the Six-Day War.

killed more Palestinian refugees and Lebanese after a 1972 terrorist attack in Israel's Tel Aviv airport, which killed forty Israelis. A few months later, during the 1972 Summer Olympics in Munich, Germany, eleven Israeli athletes were killed by a small Palestinian group called Black September. The group took its name from events in Jordan in September 1970, when the Jordanian government took military actions against Palestinian organizations in Jordan after heavy fighting, forcing Palestinian groups into Lebanese refugee camps. Israel, in retaliation for the Olympics attack, bombed refugee camps in southern Lebanon, even though most people in the camps were not members or supporters of Black September.

Lebanese citizens quickly moved out of southern Lebanon, where most of the refugee camps were located. There was too much fighting along the border. It created an upheaval in the country's business, and of course, there was little tourism to add to the economy. More and more people were becoming impoverished.

Meanwhile, the number of Palestinian refugees entering Lebanon continued to increase. This caused a great shift in the religious balance of the nation. Suddenly there were far more Muslims than Christians.

Several groups built up their own small, private armies, or militias, including the Palestine Liberation Organization (PLO) and Muslim and Christian forces. Clashes became more frequent on the streets of Beirut. All this bloodshed was a buildup to 1975, when the Lebanese Muslims and Christians would be locked in a brutal civil war.

The Palestine Liberation Organization

The Palestine Liberation Organization (PLO) began in 1964. It was a group devoted to getting back for Palestinians the land that had been lost during the 1948 Arab-Israeli War. This group was willing to use any means possible, including violence, to achieve its goals. The PLO sponsored a particularly fierce group of commandos, or *fedayeen*. The fedayeen and other splinter groups frequently tangled with forces led by Jordan's King Hussein. In 1970 the king forced more Palestinians to flee Jordan and head to Lebanon's refugee camps, which were already overburdened. People living in these tent camps fought hunger, disease, and the elements every day.

When members of the PLO ended up in these miserable camps, they took the opportunity to recruit people for the fedayeen. It was fairly easy to turn the young men of the camps, who were homeless, unemployed, and downtrodden, into commandos. Several violent raids on Israel set out from Lebanon's refugee camps. In return, Israeli bombs frequently targeted the camps. Fedayeen forces in the camps also fought against troops from the Christian-led Lebanese government. The government blamed the fedayeen and the PLO for the many innocent lives lost by people caught in the crossfire. The PLO went on to play a large role in Lebanon's brutal civil war, which began in 1975.

The Civil War Begins

The first clash of the civil war came in April 1975. A bus full of Palestinians was attacked in Beirut by a Christian militia. The PLO and the Nationalist Movement, made up of other

Muslim militias, took on the Lebanese Front, consisting of Christian militias and the government military, throughout the streets of Beirut. As the fighting continued into the following year, the Lebanese government asked neighboring Syria to send its military to stop the war. The fighting was coming to an end in 1978, but then problems erupted between the Syrian and Christian militias. This dragged on for three more years.

In 1981 a ceasefire agreement was signed, but it ended less than a year later, just as dozens of other ceasefires had fallen by the wayside in previous years. The Israeli government, wanting to get rid of the PLO for good, provoked the group in many ways. It blamed the PLO for an assassination attempt on an Israeli ambassador in London. The Israelis then dropped bombs on PLO targets in southern Lebanon. In June 1982 the bombings escalated into an invasion

Militiamen at a barricade in Beirut during the civil war in 1975

In an attempt to stop the PLO, Israel invaded Lebanon in June 1982.

of Lebanon, a retaliation to the country for hosting the PLO. As many as eighteen thousand people were killed in the invasion, most of them Lebanese but also Israelis, Palestinians, and Syrians. Finally an international force of troops from France, Great Britain, and the United States was able to bring temporary stability to the region. But this multinational force left the region in 1983 after a terrorist attack on Beirut killed three hundred French and American soldiers. The violence continued throughout Lebanon.

By 1985 the Israeli forces were slowly leaving all but southern Lebanon and preparing Christian militia groups to continue their fight. So the battles carried on among Christians, Sunnis, Druze, Shi'ites, and Palestinians. There were bombings in the cities, hostages were taken frequently, and fighting in the streets was common. Thousands were killed. The suffering of the Lebanese people grew as their country was demolished and the goods and services they needed were depleted by the war.

Though there was still a Lebanese government, it was clearly the various militias that ruled the country. Many of them were backed by foreign governments, particularly Syria,

In October 1983, terrorists attacked American headquarters in Beirut.

The Hezbollah

The attacks on the French and American soldiers were carried out by an organization known as Hezbollah, or "Party of God," a radical Shi'ite group backed by Iran. This group felt that the plight of the Shi'ites was being overlooked amid the turmoil of the war. Though the Shi'ites made up a large percentage of Lebanon's population, they were mostly poor and left out of the power struggle between Christians and Sunni Muslims. Since most Lebanese Shi'ites lived in the southern part of the country, they were the ones caught in the crossfire between Israelis and the PLO. The destruction of their villages left many Shi'ites homeless.

The Hezbollah (left) gave the Shi'ites an outlet for their anger and frustration. It also gave them increasing power, as Hezbollah proved to be a forceful fighting unit. Members were willing to die to get rid of Western influence in their land, and their suicide attacks on Israeli and American targets created a lot of fear. They also began to take hostages as a way to get publicity for their views. Today, backed by both Syria and Iran, Hezbollah continues occasional attacks on Israeli settlements in Lebanon.

Iran, Iraq, and Libya. It was sometimes difficult to sort out just which group was opposed to another and why. This mixture of political, religious, and international disagreements and hatred made the fighting in Lebanon a challenging situation to resolve.

In 1989 outsiders again tried to bring peace to Lebanon. Leaders of Morocco, Algeria, and Saudi Arabia proposed a ceasefire agreement. This was coupled with a plan that would bring some balance to Muslim and Christian representation in Lebanon's government, though the confessional distribution of roles would still be in place. Hopes for a lasting peace were growing.

The War Ends

Two years later, in 1991, Syria signed a cooperation pact with Lebanon. Much of Lebanon's land would now be controlled jointly by armies from Syria and Lebanon. Most historians note this year as the end of Lebanon's civil war. Some 150,000 lives had been lost. Damage to Lebanon, especially in Beirut, amounted to more than $25 billion. It wasn't truly the end of the fighting, though. The many rivals didn't reach agreement quickly or easily. There were still occasional bloody skirmishes on the streets. Hezbollah continued to attack Israel, and Israel retaliated by bombing southern Lebanon. A ceasefire agreement in 1996 between Hezbollah and Israel gave Syria a role in policing the activities of both groups, and the problems diminished even further.

The fighting continues sporadically, though. Hezbollah shelled Israeli posts in southern Lebanon in October 2003. Israel responded with artillery fire and air strikes into the valleys and hills surrounding Mount Hermon, where the Hezbollah hideouts are located.

Lebanon has made great strides to rebuild its cities and economy. Reconstruction of Beirut's urban center and residential areas has been fast and impressive. Not only have new buildings risen, but archeological ruins have also been carefully uncovered and put on display. Most of the groups within Lebanon's society have learned to live side by side in peace. They are working to restore the country to an international hot spot of finance and culture, as it was during the peaks of its lustrous past.

A Government Reorganized

LEBANON BECAME AN INDEPENDENT NATION IN 1943. ITS constitution was written earlier, in 1926. In it, the Lebanese people are granted many rights and personal freedoms. There shall be no state religion, the document states. A free press is guaranteed. Citizens have the ability to make changes to their government.

Lebanon's government is a parliamentary democracy. It is also unicameral, meaning there is one legislative body, or parliament, that makes laws for the nation. Lebanese people elect their parliament, called the National Assembly, every four years. All males twenty-one and older may vote, and women that age who have at least an elementary-school

Opposite: **Lebanese students display national pride.**

The seat of the Lebanese Parliament is in Beirut in the Grand Serail.

Lebanon's Flag

The focal point of Lebanon's national flag is the Lebanese cedar tree, symbolic of the country's history, holiness, and desire for peace. The flag is lined with broad red stripes at the top and the bottom, symbolizing sacrifice.

education may also vote. Every six years, members of the National Assembly elect a president. The president selects the nation's prime minister.

Restoring the Government

Today, more than a decade after its civil war ended, Lebanon is rebuilding its political systems. Elections are held on schedule, and all citizens are given greater rights under the law. For many years, though, the government of Lebanon had to struggle to maintain any control over the country.

Throughout much of the 1970s and '80s, several militias were at war in the country. Their constant warring made it impossible for the Lebanese government to do much but react to the mayhem and try to keep vital services available to its citizens. The Lebanese government itself played a role in the conflicts, through its military and its support of controversial policies, especially confessionalism, which many people felt was unfair.

There have been a few updates to confessionalism. In 1989 the Ta'if Agreement was passed. It put into law the National Pact that until then had been an unwritten agreement, mandating that certain seats in parliament be held by Christians and Muslims. It also gave greater powers to the prime minister and the speaker of the National Assembly, making their roles nearly as important as that of the president.

Leadership Roles

The president holds a great deal of power in Lebanon. This individual is in charge of making official any laws passed by

Lebanon's head of state is President Emile Lahoud.

the National Assembly. He can also create additional regulations to ensure that the laws are kept. In addition, the president negotiates all treaties with other nations. The president selects a prime minister for Lebanon, but the National Assembly must approve the choice. Emile Lahoud is the current president of Lebanon.

The prime minister must sign any of the legislation that the president signs. He also chooses the cabinet members, though he consults with the president and National Assembly members on his selections. Cabinet members guide the president and the prime minister on specific topics.

Rafiq Hariri

Rafiq Hariri is the current prime minister of Lebanon, a post he held from 1992 to 1998 and again since 2000. He serves along with President Emile Lahoud.

Hariri was born in Sidon in 1944 and attended schools there, later graduating from the Beirut Arab University. After a brief career in Lebanon as an accountant, Hariri moved to Saudi Arabia, where he became a successful businessman with his own construction firm. He also worked in the real-estate and banking industries and became quite wealthy. He is known not just as a good businessman but also as a philanthropist, one who donates money to charity. During Lebanon's civil war Hariri paid for several educational and social projects in his homeland. He built schools and a hospital and provided funding for poor students to attend universities.

During the 1980s, Hariri worked to help bring an end to the war and was instrumental in writing the Ta'if Agreement of 1989. When he was named prime minister in 1992 he also took on the role of finance minister and directed much of the country's rebuilding. Hariri established the Ministry of the Affairs of Displaced

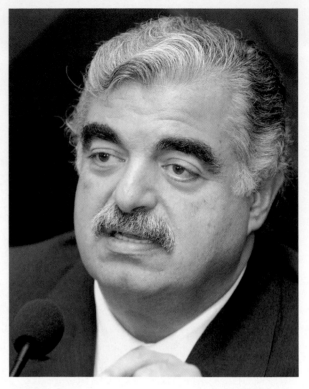

People, which enabled several thousand Lebanese refugees to return to the homes they'd fled during the war. He has been one of the primary people plotting Lebanon's path since the end of the country's civil war.

Most of the nation's legislative power rests with the National Assembly. This group consists of 128 members. Members are elected based on their religious affiliations, and they form political groups based on that. They don't represent political parties as most politicians in the United States and Canada do. Each year they meet twice for three months at a time. When they vote on legislation, their votes must be public. This group is responsible for creating a budget for the country and levying taxes on the citizens.

The Judicial System

Lebanon's legal system is influenced by those of several other cultures, particularly those that have had a hand in ruling the country at some point in its history. Napoleonic code from France has been a factor, as has Ottoman law. Canon law, the body of rules covering practices of members of a Christian church, has influenced Lebanon's legal system, too.

There are many layers to the nation's court system. Most cases are heard in civilian courts covering commercial, civil, and criminal law. There is also a military court and courts called tribunals, affiliated with Lebanon's various religions. These tribunals decide such matters as divorce and child custody. There are no juries in any of these courts, but defendants may appeal decisions.

Cases involving a threat to Lebanon's national security go before the Judicial Council, made up of five senior judges. Defendants here may not appeal the verdict.

Lebanon's Constitutional Court rules on the constitutionality of new laws. Finally, cases involving Lebanon's president or prime minister are heard by the Supreme Council.

NATIONAL GOVERNMENT OF LEBANON

Legislative Branch

PRESIDENT

PRIME MINISTER

CABINET MEMBERS

NATIONAL ASSEMBLY (128 MEMBERS)

Judicial Branch

JUDICIAL COUNCIL (5 MEMBERS)

CONSTITUTIONAL COURT

SUPREME COUNCIL

Beirut: Did You Know This?

Beirut, with its population of 1,171,000, is Lebanon's capital. The city has shaken off the dust and the dirt of some fifteen years of bombing during the country's civil war. Today it's flourishing with scores of new buildings, parks, homes, and streets. It is aiming to recapture its glory as the cultural center that had been known as the Paris of the Middle East.

Situated about halfway along Lebanon's border with the Mediterranean Sea, on the tip of a little parcel of land that juts out into the water, Beirut is in a great spot for trade. Ships have stopped there for centuries. In fact, the earliest settlements on the land that is now Beirut date back to more than five thousand years ago. In 1400 B.C. it was a Phoenician city named Beroth, meaning "the city of wells." Later, in the first century B.C., it was known as Berytus, another early version of its modern name. At that time it was controlled by the Romans. It later fell under the control of the various conquering nations that held Lebanon during its history. Each nation influenced the city and its culture, helping it to achieve its status as a home to great businessmen, skilled craftsmen, and talented intellectuals.

Today Beirut is home to several universities that train top students from throughout the Middle East. There are numerous banks and trading operations. It has several museums and many restaurants, too. It is a major tourist destination.

There are many highlights for visitors to Beirut. Perhaps top on the list would be the National Museum. Though it was heavily damaged during the civil war, and many of its artifacts were stolen, it was one of the first structures rebuilt in the city. Reopened in 1999, it contains many

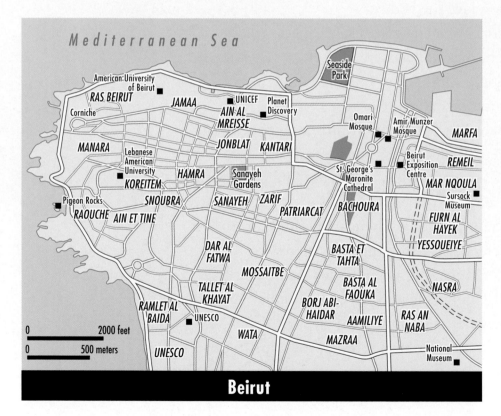

exhibits outlining the country's history, dating back to 2000 B.C. Other popular museums include Planet Discovery, a children's museum; the Sursock Museum, showing the works of modern Lebanese artists; and the archeological museum at the American University of Beirut, with highlights including Phoenician glassware and other crafts.

Archeological remains can be found throughout the city, including the remains of a Roman bath; part of the Roman Basilica, the foundations of a castle from the Crusades; and the Amir Munzer Mosque, built in 1620.

The greatest natural beauty in Beirut is found at Pigeon Rocks (below), natural rock arches just offshore along Beirut's Corniche, or seaside walkway. Visitors can enjoy lovely hiking trails and pretty scenery.

Foreign Relations

Lebanon shares most of its land border with Syria, and it is with this nation that it maintains its closest ties. The countries signed an agreement calling for cooperation in 1991. This came two years after the Ta'if Agreement, which stated that "Lebanon is linked to Syria by distinctive ties deriving strength from kinship, history, and common interests." Since then, the two countries have signed several more agreements, striving to increase cooperation. Syria keeps military forces activated throughout Lebanon, however, and some in Lebanon are opposed to this.

Lebanon is on good terms with most of the other Arab nations. It has trade agreements with nearly all of them even though there have been tensions in the past with such countries as Iraq and Libya. The government works to make sure that Lebanon keeps strong ties with other Muslim countries, too. It is a member of the Organization of Islamic Conference. The European Union also has a trade agreement with Lebanon.

Lebanon's most strained relationship is with the neighboring nation of Israel. Bombings and other attacks between Israelis and members of Hezbollah living in southern Lebanon continue periodically. There have been several attempts at peace treaties, often including Syria, the United States, and France. Though the fighting has not come to a stop, the level of violence has decreased in recent years. Many Lebanese are hopeful that the end will come soon and that residents will be able to live in peace.

Syrian troops are active in Lebanon. Here tanks are repositioned near Tripoli.

Economic Rebound

As with many other things in Lebanon, the nation's economy is recovering following the civil war. With each year that passes the situation improves. The government has reorganized and begun collecting taxes and regulating businesses. Foreign investors are willing to take a risk in Lebanon once again, and people are not afraid to live their normal lives. Businesses are doing much better.

Lebanon has a free-market economy, which means that the government does not control pricing and trade. Service businesses, especially banking and tourism, bring about 70 percent of the money into the country's economy. Industry brings in another 20 percent, while agriculture accounts for the other 10 percent.

Banking

Lebanon has been a center of banking in the Middle East for decades. One reason is that until 2001, the country's laws required secrecy in banking. Money could move easily through the system with few restrictions. This freedom attracted money from wealthy foreign individuals and banks outside the country.

Opposite: **Lebanon's economy has been one of growth since the end of the civil war.**

Banking is an important business in Lebanon. This is a banking center building in Beirut.

Lebanese Currency

The basic unit of Lebanese currency is the Lebanese pound. It takes 100 paisters to equal one pound. As of September 2004, 1,514.00 Lebanese pounds equaled U.S.$1.

Banks notes in Lebanon are colorful and decorative. Some display drawings of native plants, while others include intricate designs and graphics.

The Lebanese government borrowed money from Lebanese banks to rebuild such things as roads, schools, and hospitals. Today it is working to repay those debts. Many businesses once owned by the government, such as shipping ports, electric utilities, water suppliers, and airlines, have been sold to private investors. The money paid for them helps pay the country's debts and build the economy.

Tourism

Opposite: **Tourism in Lebanon has been on the rise since war's end. Here visitors tour the Roman Temple of Jupiter in Baalbek.**

Tourists are coming back to Lebanon, eager to relax on its sunny beaches, ski down its slopes, and appreciate its many historical sites. These tourists bring in money that makes up a large portion of Lebanon's economy. This business is one of the main reasons the country was so eager to rebuild following

the civil war. Virtually no tourists arrived during the years of fighting, and the Lebanese want everyone to forget the troubles that kept people away.

Today there is plenty to draw visitors and keep them occupied. All major cities offer a range of hotels, from inexpensive to lavish. For the more adventurous visitors, companies offer hiking trips into the mountains. They can take bicycle tours or explore caves. People also enjoy traveling to villages to celebrate some of the annual festivals they hold. Lebanon is noted for delicious foods, another attraction. More than a half-million people visit Lebanon each year. Most travel from elsewhere in the Middle East, from Europe, and from the United States.

What Lebanon Grows, Makes, and Mines	
Agriculture (2001 est.)	
Citrus	397,000 metric tons
Tomatoes	336,000 metric tons
Potatoes	260,000 metric tons
Manufacturing	
Cement (2001 est.)	2,700,000 metric tons
Metals	80,000 metric tons
Clothing/Textiles	$335 million
Mining	
Limestone	40,000 metric tons
Salt	3,500 metric tons
Gypsum	3,000 metric tons

Industry

The main industrial products in Lebanon are clothing, processed foods, aluminum products, pharmaceuticals and chemicals, cement, and jewelry. Most of this production takes place in or around Beirut. Cement production takes place near Tripoli. Many of the products are sold to other countries. Most of these exports go to France, Switzerland, the United States, Saudi Arabia, and the United Arab Emirates.

Centuries ago Lebanon had a flourishing forestry industry. But the Lebanese cedars and many other forest areas are now nearly gone. There is a small commercial forestry industry, though, where trees are planted specifically to be cut someday for lumber. There is very little mining done. A few operations quarry gypsum and limestone.

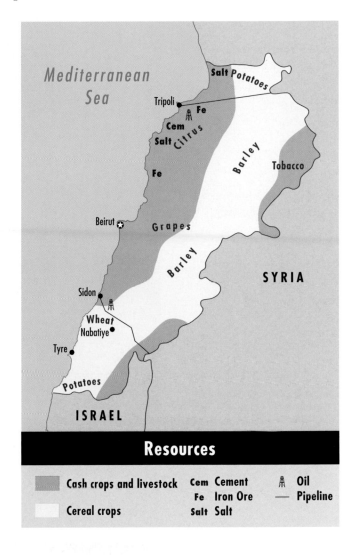

Agriculture

About one-fifth of Lebanon's land is used for agriculture, mostly in the Bekaa Valley. This region doesn't get a lot of rainfall, but because it lies between two mountain ranges, there is a good deal of runoff into rivers flowing through the valley. Farmers use irrigation to get the water to their crops.

Agriculture was once a major part of Lebanon's economy. For centuries, farmers worked hard to terrace the mountain-

Grapes from the fertile Bekaa Valley produce top wines.

slopes, providing even more space for growing food to feed the nation. Today, agriculture makes up only about 10 percent of Lebanon's economy.

Grapes grown in the Bekaa Valley are one of Lebanon's top agricultural products. Some of these grapes are used by Lebanon's award-winning wine producers. Other products grown in the Bekaa Valley include potatoes, tomatoes, and tobacco. Grains, especially wheat and barley, are grown here, too, but these are not the major products they once were. During the Roman occupation, the Bekaa Valley helped to feed the entire Roman Empire. The region is not as fertile as it once was, though, due to overfarming through the centuries.

Orchards line the valley at slightly higher elevations, growing apples, olives, peaches, figs, cherries, and plums. Fruits are grown along Lebanon's warm and sunny coast, especially citrus, bananas, melons, and strawberries.

Some farmers raise animals, including poultry, goats, sheep, cattle, pigs, and horses. There are a few commercial fishers who sell mostly to the local markets. Trout are caught from rivers in the Bekaa Valley, and other seafood comes from the Mediterranean Sea.

Lebanon's economy has made great strides since the war years. Banking, tourism, manufacturing, and agriculture have grown in the years of stability. If the country can continue to keep the peace, so that people feel comfortable visiting and investing their money, Lebanon's economic future should be bright.

System of Weights and Measures

The standard system of weights and measures in Lebanon is the metric system.

The People of Lebanon

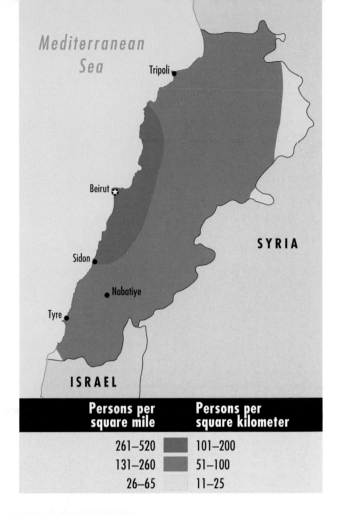

The Lebanese population is a mix of people from many backgrounds. Over the centuries, numerous nations have conquered the land. Each time, some foreigners stayed behind. Greeks, Egyptians, Assyrians, and more have become part of the fabric of the Lebanese people, contributing to the gene pool as well as adding culture and traditions.

Due to the political climate of the country, Lebanon's first and last official national census was held in 1932. A 2003 estimate by the U.S. Central

Persons per square mile		Persons per square kilometer	
261–520		101–200	
131–260		51–100	
26–65		11–25	

A crowded street in Beirut

Opposite: **The Lebanese are a mix of peoples from the past.**

The People of Lebanon **83**

Ethnic Breakdown of Lebanese Population

Arab	95%
Armenian	4%
Multiethnic ancestry	1%

Intelligence Agency puts the current population at 3,727,703. Almost half live in Beirut.

Ancestry

Though Lebanese citizens' ancestries vary, nearly all of them are Arab. Four percent are Armenian, another 1 percent are of multiethnic ancestry, and 95 percent are Arab, though some Christians refer to themselves as Phoenicians. Arab ancestry is well represented in the appearance of the people. In general, Lebanese have dark hair, with dark eyes and high cheekbones.

Most Armenians arrived in Lebanon during World War I after fleeing Turkey to escape the genocide. It is their offspring who now make up Lebanon's largest minority group. Most live at Beirut's eastern edge.

There are many Lebanese people living in other countries around the world. Some estimates say at least 10 million Lebanese and people of Lebanese descent live outside of Lebanon. They typically maintain close ties with family members who remain in Lebanon, often sending money. Millions of dollars are added to the nation's economy this way.

At the same time, a large number of foreigners live in Lebanon, most of them doing menial labor, construction, and farm jobs throughout the country. The majority come from Syria, but others are from Ethiopia, Sri Lanka, and Egypt.

Population of Lebanon's Largest Cities (2003 est.)

Beirut	1,171,000
Tripoli	212,900
Sidon	149,000
Tyre	117,100
Nabatiye	89,400

Traditions and Values

The most important thing to nearly every Lebanese is family. Loyalty is highly valued and expected. Lebanese people are

Palestinians in Lebanon

Many of Lebanon's Arabs who aren't Lebanese are Palestinian. Their actual numbers are uncertain, but estimates place the total at about 350,000. Though most have lived in Lebanon for at least fifty years, they aren't widely accepted by others in the country. Palestinians are resented for the role they played in Lebanon's civil war. They are restricted from taking most jobs, so they depend on aid from the United Nations to provide for their needs. Most live in severe poverty, often crowded together in refugee camps. Even though most Lebanese would like the Palestinians to leave, and many Palestinians would like to leave, their options are limited. Since Palestine no longer exists, and since the areas that might become a Palestinian state in the future are under Israeli control, Palestinians do not have a country of their own.

loyal not only to their close family members but also to members of their large, extended clan.

Warmth and respect are evident even in simple greetings. Visitors to a family home are often told *"Ahlan wu sahlan,"* meaning "You have come among family," basically stating that the guests are welcomed and safe. In farewell, Lebanese people may say *"Allah ma'ak,"* which means "Good luck." When talking with one other, especially when the discussion is on emotional subjects, Lebanese people will often take time before speaking. It's important for them to express themselves carefully so that their intentions are not misunderstood.

Body Language

Two men greet each other as a sign of friendship.

When Lebanese people greet each other they often are very formal and spend a good bit of time on ritual. It is customary for them to shake hands and give a friendly, courteous nod toward each other. A man may tip his hat toward a woman or place his right hand flat upon his chest, while she will nod politely or place her right hand on her chest. Men frequently pat other men on the back to signal friendship. Close friends and relatives may give each other a small embrace or a kiss on the cheek.

In Lebanon people's sense of personal space is smaller than in the United States and Canada. Friends stand closer to each other than they do in the Western world. They often use bold gestures when speaking. Raising the hand with the palm outward indicates "no." Another way to signal "no" is to move the head up while raising the eyebrows. A simple nod means "yes." Shaking the head from side to side is a sign of a lack of understanding rather than of disagreement, as it would be in North America. Showing the soles of one's shoes to another is impolite. It is also rude to raise a closed fist in the air.

It's common to see Lebanese men carrying strings of beads, known as prayer beads. Each bead has printed on it one of the names or qualities of God. Sometimes they are also used as worry beads. These are a simple way to help relieve stress. Men will often twist the beads and twirl them together while walking, in meetings, and at other times when they are thinking and trying to work out issues in their minds.

Prayer beads are a common sight among Muslim men.

French and English are spoken in Lebanon, as well as Arabic.

The Arabic Language

Lebanese people speak Arabic, though French is also commonly used. English, too, is fairly common. Many Lebanese people learn to speak two or more languages.

It is nearly impossible to write Arabic words with the Roman alphabet that is used for English. There are sounds in Arabic that are not represented by Roman letters. One sound, for example, is formed deep in the throat, with air pushed out while the throat muscles are tightened. Another sound is a deep, fast breathing sound similar to the noise made when people blow on their glasses to clean them.

Several methods have been devised to try to re-create the sounds of Arabic words, but none are perfect. That's why you often see several different spellings of common Arabic terms. Islam's holy book may be spelled *Qur'an* or *Koran*, for example, and *Muhammad* is sometimes *Mohammed*, among other spellings.

There are twenty-eight Arabic letters, twenty-five of which are consonants. Of the remaining three, two of them can sometimes

Common Arabic Words and Phrases

as-salamu :alai-kum	hello (Literally, "Peace be with you")
wa :alai-kum as-salaam	reply to hello
al-Hamdu li-l-aáah	praise be to God
sabaah al-khair	good morning
sabaah an-nuur	reply to good morning
masa' al-khair	good evening
masaa an-nuur	reply to good evening
shukran	thank you
asif	I am sorry

work as consonants, too. Each letter is written slightly differently, depending on whether it comes at the beginning, the middle, or the end of a word. Each written letter has its own distinct sound.

When Arabic is written, it goes from right to left, opposite to the way English is written. Most letters in a word connect in a flowing style to those next to them. There is no distinction in Arabic between uppercase and lowercase letters, as there is in English.

The same form of Arabic is used for printed materials in all Arabic-speaking nations. Lebanese people and other Arab speakers can pick up books, magazines, and newspapers written in any country throughout the Arab world and easily read them. It is just one of the ways that Lebanese people, and other Arabs, stay in touch.

A bank sign in Arabic and French

A Religious Land

RELIGION PLAYS AN IMPORTANT role in the culture of Lebanon and the lives of its people. When the Bible speaks of "the land of milk and honey," it is Lebanon. Many faiths are followed there, played out in a variety of mosques, churches, and temples; in private, quiet rituals, and in bold, public worships.

The religious lives of Lebanese people today reflect the many influences brought to Lebanon during past centuries. Islam and Christianity are Lebanon's chief religions, but within each of these are several versions, or denominations.

Most Lebanese people are Muslims, followers of Islam. About half of all Lebanese Muslims are Shi'ite Muslims, while most of the rest are Sunni. Some are Druze, an official off-shoot of Shi'ite Islam. Though each has its distinctive teachings, there are similarities among all these versions of Islam.

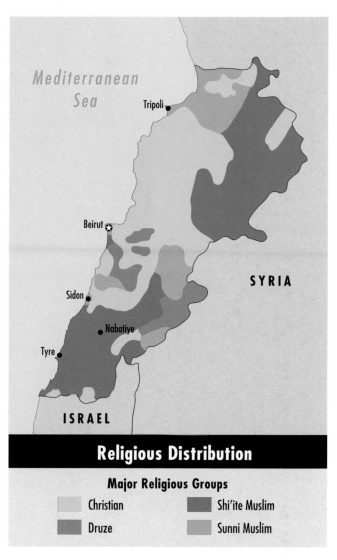

Religious Distribution

Major Religious Groups

Christian	Shi'ite Muslim
Druze	Sunni Muslim

Opposite. Prayer and worship takes place at mosques throughout Lebanon. Islam is Lebanon's chief religion.

Thirty percent of Lebanese are Christians. Here a Maronite priest celebrates Easter.

Lebanese also observe several Christian faiths. There are Catholic, Protestant, and Orthodox churches. A small number of Lebanese people observe the Jewish faith.

Islam

Islam is the religion with the largest following in Lebanon. The word *Islam* comes from the Arabic word *salaama*, which means "submission to God and his will." Followers are called Muslims, a word meaning "one who submits." They are obedient to the will of God, who is called Allah in Arabic. This is the same God who is worshiped by Christians and Jews around the world.

The prophet Muhammad founded Islam around A.D. 610. At that time, he was forty years old, living in the city of

Major Religions Observed in Lebanon

Muslim	69%
Christian	30%
Jewish	1%

Mecca, located in what is now Saudi Arabia. Muslims believe that he was visited by the archangel Gabriel, who told Muhammad about the "word of God," explaining how people should live, what they should believe, and the way they should worship. The archangel continued to appear to Muhammad throughout the rest of his life, each time bringing new messages from God. Muhammad felt the responsibility to share his vision, and beginning in A.D. 613 he spoke the word of God to the people around him. Eventually these messages were written down in the Muslim holy book, the Qur'an.

Muhammad in Mecca

Muhammad and his teachings were not immediately accepted. He attracted only a few dozen followers in his early years. Most people already had their own spiritual beliefs and practices. They were furious with Muhammad for attacking the idols they worshiped. The wealthy and powerful people in Mecca did not like Muhammad's statement that Allah was the one deity, nor did they wish to share their wealth with those in poverty, as Muhammad said Allah demanded. When those who opposed Muhammad's message threatened his life, he realized he had to leave

Mecca. In A.D. 622, he and his small group of followers fled north to the oasis town of Medina.

This journey became known as the *Hejira*, or migration, and 622 marks the beginning of the Islamic calendar. In Medina, Muhammad found people who were much more open to his teachings about the word of God. He rapidly became a successful religious leader. In a few years he had thousands of followers. He gathered a force of ten thousand soldiers in A.D. 630 and led them to his former home of Mecca. There they attacked the idols people had worshiped and turned the population to Islam. Mecca was reestablished as a holy city.

Muhammad died just two years later, in 632, but Islam continued to thrive. His successors were known as *caliphs*, which comes from *khalifat rasul Allah*. This means "successor of the messenger of God." They continued to share Muhammad's messages and saw to it that the word of God was shared with people in distant lands. Islam spread across all of Arabia within two years, and in ten years it was well established in Lebanon, as well as in Egypt, Palestine, and Syria. Still, there were problems among the faithful.

The Islamic Calendar

The Islamic calendar is a lunar calendar, meaning that it is determined by the phases of the moon. A month on this calendar is the period of time between two new moons. It is different from the Gregorian calendar used throughout most of the world, which is based on the solar year. Muslims follow both calendars, with the Islamic calendar determining their holy days. While the solar calendar has 365 days a year, there are 354 days in the Islamic calendar, so Muslim holidays fall 11 days earlier each year. The beginning of the first month of the year is Ras as-Sana, the Muslim New Year. This day commemorates the beginning of Islamic history, the day in 622 when Muhammad began the Hejira, leaving Mecca for Medina.

The Shi'ites and the Sunnis

After the death of Muhammad, Islam split into two main sects, which eventually became the Shi'ites and the Sunnis. Muhammad did not name a successor before he died. Muslims disagreed over who should take over as caliph, the leader of the faith. The two most likely candidates were Ali, Muhammad's cousin and the husband of his daughter Fatima, and Abu Bakr, the father of Muhammad's second wife. Supporters for Abu Bakr finally got their man into the role as the first caliph. Two more followed him, and then Ali became the fourth caliph, serving until his assassination in 661.

Ali's supporters continued to believe that he was the legitimate successor of Muhammad. They were referred to as belonging to the *shi at Ali*, or part of Ali. Today we call them Shias or Shi'ites. They believe that a true leader of Islam should be a direct descendent of Muhammad. They expect a spiritual leader will eventually emerge to form an empire based on their beliefs.

Sunnis accept the legitimacy of the line of caliphs who have succeeded Muhammad over the centuries. They believe that any leader who follows *Sharia*, the law of the Muslims, with fairness deserves Muslim support.

Despite these disagreements, the two sects agree on most other aspects of Islam. Throughout the world today there are more than 1 billion Muslims. Most live in the Middle East, Africa, and Asia, but their numbers are growing in the United States, Europe, and Canada as well.

The Druze

The Druze began as an offshoot of Shi'ite Islam, but today many Muslims don't consider the Druze faith to

be a true version of Islam. The Druze formed in the eleventh century when their leader, Muhammad bin Asmail ad Darazi, declared that the Muslim caliph at the time, al Hakim bin Amrillah, was divine, or God in the form of a human. Followers today still pray to Hakim and look forward to the day he will reappear. They believe that there is a fixed number of souls that are reincarnated in people over and over again. Absolute truth with each other is an important aspect of Druze behavior; however, they are permitted to lie to outsiders, especially regarding matters of their faith. They strive to keep their faith private. This secrecy has helped them avoid persecution. It has also made it difficult to attract new members, since few outsiders know much about the faith. Today the Druze keep their faith going only by keeping the children of their members involved.

Sunnis are the majority throughout the Middle East. In Lebanon, however, most Muslims are Shi'ites, though there are Sunnis, and a smaller group called Druze.

The Beliefs of Islam

Islam is based on teachings from many prophets, people Muslims believe were chosen by Allah to speak for him. Some prophets, such as Moses and Abraham, are found in the Old Testament. Jesus, they believe, was a great prophet, too, though they don't believe that he was the son of God as Christians do. Muhammad's teachings, they believe, are the most complete and accurate of all the prophet's teachings.

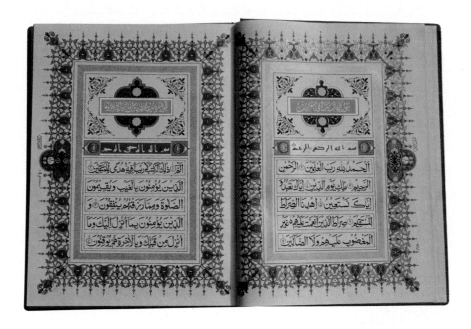

The Qur'an teaches the principles of Islam.

Allah has given humans all the guidance necessary to live on the correct spiritual path, Muslims believe, and these principles are recorded in the Qur'an. Those who follow Allah's teachings will enter heaven when they die, while those who are disobedient in life are doomed to an eternity of punishment in hell.

The Pillars of Islam

Just as the pillars of a building give it strength and structure, so do the Five Pillars of Islam give structure to the lives of Muslims.

The first pillar of Islam is *shahada*, or witnessing. Muslims must make a public statement of faith. They say a verse in Arabic that translates to "I bear witness that there is no God but Allah, and Muhammad is the messenger of God." They must declare this with genuine belief.

The second pillar of Islam is prayer.

Salat, or prayer, is the second pillar of Islam. Muslims are obliged to pray five times each day, at dawn, at noon, in midafternoon, at sunset, and in the evening. Muslims believe that prayer is not needed by Allah, for he has no needs. Instead, prayer exists as a benefit to humans, helping us to develop strong, spiritual personalities.

The third pillar of Islam is *zakat*, or charity. Muslims are obliged to share their money with those in need, including the poor, new converts to Islam, Muslim prisoners of war, and foreigners seeking help.

Sawm, or fasting, is the fourth pillar of Islam. Muslims abstain completely from eating, drinking, and smoking throughout all daylight hours during Ramadan, the ninth month of the Muslim calendar. To Muslims it is an act of worship that instills in them a sense of devotion, willpower, moderation, discipline, maturity, and unity.

The final pillar is *hajj*. This is the requirement that every Muslim make a pilgrimage, or visit, to Mecca at least once in his or her lifetime, if at all possible. Pilgrims wear a white robe and pray at the Great Mosque in Mecca. Hajj should take place during the first or second week of the Muslim month of Zuul-Hijja. Millions of Muslims participate each year, making hajj the world's largest annual convention of faith.

Millions of Muslims travel to Mecca in Saudi Arabia to pray at the Great Mosque.

Christians light candles at Saint Michael's Church in Beirut.

Christianity

Lebanon has played a major role in the geography of Christianity since the religion's earliest days. The faith is based on the life and teachings of Jesus as described in the New Testament. Many of Jesus' followers traveled to Lebanon to spread his message. Saint Paul frequently stayed in Lebanon, preaching to crowds that would gather. Today beautiful churches and chapels, many hundreds of years old, are the centers for Christian worship.

Jesus Christ lived some two thousand years ago. He began preaching in Palestine, near Lebanon, traveling through the region with twelve followers, also known as disciples and apostles. Jesus performed some of his miracles in Lebanon, according to stories in the New Testament. He healed the daughter of a Phoenician woman and turned water into wine at a wedding in Cana, a town southeast of Tyre. Jesus and his followers spoke about the kingdom of heaven and proclaimed to all their listeners that Jesus was the Messiah, sent as the Son of God to be king of the Jews. Jesus preached about justice for all people, telling listeners that they were all members of one brotherhood and should have mercy on each other.

Just as Muhammad's message centuries later would anger those in power, so did Jesus' words. The Roman leaders of the time were infuriated by his claim to be king of the Jews. This claim amounted to treason, they asserted, and they feared he would lead an uprising against their authority. To prevent this, they put Jesus to death, crucifying him.

The New Testament tells that Jesus turned water into wine.

Though Jesus' followers were fearful following his death, they quickly resumed their work of spreading his message. They were eager to report that three days after his death, they witnessed that he had come back to life. This belief that Jesus rose from the dead—called the Resurrection—is one of the basic aspects of Christianity.

The first followers of Christ had been born Jewish. Over time, though, their faith evolved into a religion of its own, and they became known as Christians. The apostles and others helped the spread of Christianity, which has grown throughout the centuries to become the world's largest religion.

Throughout those centuries, there have been divisions among Christians, just as Muslims divided into separate groups. In the 800s there were rivalries between Christian leaders in Rome and leaders in Constantinople, now Istanbul, Turkey. This led to Christianity's separation into the Roman Catholic Church and the Eastern Orthodox Church in 1054.

Further divisions came in the 1500s. Protests over matters of faith and authority led many Roman Catholics to break away from their church. They became known as Protestants and have since divided into several denominations.

The Maronite Church is the main Christian faith observed in Lebanon. It is one of the several versions of Catholicism followed there. The country's other Christian religions include Eastern Orthodox and Protestantism.

The Maronite monastery of Saint Antoine

Holy Days in Lebanon

Since Lebanon has large Muslim and Christian populations, Lebanese people observe many holy days. The holy days observed by Muslims are

Ras as-Sana, or New Year's Day	First day of Islamic calendar
Ashura	10 Moharran
Moulid an-Nabi	12 Rabi'al-Awal
Ramadan	Ninth month of the Islamic calendar
Eid al-Fitr	End of Ramadan
Eid al-Adha	10th–13th of twelfth month of Islamic calendar

The holy days observed by Christians are

Feast of Saint Maron	February 9
Holy Week	March or April
Easter	March or April
Christmas	December 25

The Maronite Church

The Maronite Church is a sect of the Roman Catholic Church. It was inspired by a fourth-century monk, Saint Maron, who lived in Syria. A religious and charismatic figure, Maron founded a monastery that he dedicated to God. He spent much of his time there in prayer. More than eight hundred monks joined his monastery and joined him as he preached his strong beliefs to those in the Syrian countryside. Following his death, a sanctuary was built over his tomb. This grew into a large monastery, and monks and missionaries went out from there to convert people to the Catholic Church.

Followers from throughout the region, including Lebanon, joined the Maronite church. During the seventh century, however, Maron's followers separated into their own group.

Cardinal Nasrallah Pierre Sfeir, Antioch and all the East

The mountains of Lebanon offered safety and free worship to Maronites. Monks worshipped as they wished in the Saint Antoine caves.

They disagreed with leaders of the Catholic Church about certain beliefs. This separation lasted some five hundred years, until they rejoined the Catholic Church in the twelfth century, coming back under the rule of the pope. Though the pope became their main religious leader, Maronites also organized under a leader called the patriarch of Antioch and all the East, who lives in Lebanon.

Lebanon, especially its mountainous region, has long played an important role in the history of the Maronites. During times of religious persecution, many Maronites fled into the mountains to avoid being captured. The mountains offered

them safety and a measure of independence. There they were free to worship as they wished, without any interference.

Today Maronites are free to worship as they wish throughout Lebanon. There are few obvious differences between the Maronite and the Roman Catholic churches today.

Torn Apart by Faith

Since its civil war ended, Lebanon and its citizens have struggled to overcome the differences that caused the terrible divisions. Many of these differences stemmed from the variety of beliefs held by Lebanese people. Most Lebanese cling to their own traditions and beliefs while peacefully allowing others to observe their own faiths. This kind of tolerance will be required of Lebanese citizens in the future, too, as they strive to live together in peace.

Lebanese Saints

Many holy people from Lebanon have been canonized as saints over the centuries. These are people the Catholic Church proclaims to be holy and close to God in heaven, based on miracles performed in their names following their deaths. Many of Lebanon's saints lived long ago, such as Saint Aquilina, born in Byblos in 281. Other saints have lived in more recent times.

Saint Charbel was born in 1828 in the mountains of Lebanon to a poor Maronite family. As a youngster he tended the family cows. While doing this, he was inspired by the beautiful scenery around him and spent his time in prayer. When he grew older he joined a monastery. He was very devout, giving up many of life's comforts to dedicate himself to God. He lived as a hermit, sleeping on the ground, eating little, and spending most of his time in prayer. He died in 1898, and during the decades that followed many miracles were attributed to him: blind people were said to have regained their sight, tumors were healed, illnesses were cured. Charbel became a saint in 1977.

Another popular Lebanese saint is Saint Rafka, born an only child in Hemlaya in 1832. She became a nun and prayed for suffering, believing it would bring her closer to God. Sister Rafka suffered from many illnesses, but still continued to work and pray with the others in her convent. She died in 1914 and became a saint in 2001.

Combining Cultures

CHAPTER

NINE

106

LEBANESE CULTURE IS, IN MANY WAYS, COMPARABLE TO the cultures of other Arab countries, but there are some striking differences. Many Middle Eastern nations are almost completely Muslim, and this religious faith dominates the art, music, and literature of their people. In Lebanon, however, there is a large percentage of Christians and some people of other faiths, so its culture is inspired by many traditions.

Also, because Lebanon is situated along the coast, it has received visitors from other lands throughout its history. The natural warmth and willingness of the Lebanese people to learn new things has made it possible for them to soak up cultural influences from many other nations, such as Greece, Turkey, and France. Literature, music, and architecture from these lands were welcomed into the Lebanese lifestyle, forming a culture unique in the world.

Opposite: **The Temple of Jupiter is a wonderful display of Roman architecture in Lebanon.**

Literature

The written word has had great respect in Lebanon, where poetry and literature are enjoyed by many. During the 1800s the Lebanese rediscovered many ancient Arab writers and brought them to the attention of the Arab world. Their stories and poems entertained new generations of readers.

Modern poetry includes a popular social form called *zajal*. Groups of poets, in front of an audience, come up with humorous songs, creating a dialogue among the groups. Novels are

Kahlil Gibran

Kahlil Gibran wrote the well-known masterpiece *The Prophet*. Gibran was a novelist, poet, and artist, perhaps the most famous writer from Lebanon. He was born in 1883 in Bcharré, in the mountains of northern Lebanon. His family was poor, and his father was sent to prison for not paying taxes. His mother was nonetheless determined to provide a good life for her children. She moved the family to America in 1895, and they settled in Boston. Gibran, who was twelve, began

learning English as soon as he started school, two months after arriving. He caught his teachers' attention quickly with his ability to draw, a hobby he'd enjoyed in Lebanon. Gibran enjoyed other artistic pursuits, too; he was drawn to Boston's opera, theater, and art museums. His teachers encouraged him to pursue a career in the arts.

Gibran returned to Lebanon in 1898 to attend Beirut University and studied classical Arabic. He later moved to Paris and then to New York City in 1912, but he remained a Lebanese citizen. Though he first earned fame for his drawings and paintings, it was his written work that earned him fans around the world. Most of his early works were written in Arabic, but he later began writing in English. He explored Christian mysticism through his writing, but he also wrote about his homeland of Lebanon. In 1920 he founded a society for Arab writers. He died in 1931 at the age of 48, and his body was returned to Lebanon, where it lies in a casket in the Gibran Museum in Bcharré.

Among Gibran's works are *The Procession, Mirrors of the Soul,* and *The Broken Wings.* His most famous work, *The Prophet,* has been translated into some twenty languages. In twenty-six poetic essays it tells the story of a traveler who teaches about life. Following World War I, Gibron wrote an essay entitled "You Have Your Lebanon and I Have My Lebanon." In it he wrote, "Verily, I say to you that an olive plant in the hills of Lebanon will outlast all of your deeds and your works; that the wooden plow pulled by the oxen in the crannies of Lebanon is nobler than your dreams and aspirations."

important, too. Emily Nasrallah, who lives in Beirut, is a writer and activist who has written several novels about the lives of ordinary Lebanese during the civil war. Among the other award-winning Lebanese writers popular today are journalist and novelist Amin Maalouf and Hanan Al-Shaykh, who details contemporary life in Lebanon.

Award-winning author Amin Maalouf

Music

Music has long played an important role in Lebanese culture. Folk songs, sung for centuries, are still enjoyed today. The tunes typically have complex rhythms and lyrics with many layers. Small groups of families and friends often will sing together for entertainment. Many times someone will

The oud is a traditional stringed instrument played in Lebanon.

accompany them on an *oud*, a stringed instrument shaped like a pear and played by plucking it with a quill. The *qanun* is also a stringed instrument, shaped like a trapezoid, with eighty-one strings. Other traditional Lebanese instruments include the *nay*, an open-ended single-reed pipe, and the *tabla*, a percussion instrument made of wood, metal, or clay and covered with taut animal skin.

Music performed with these traditional instruments is typically accompanied with

Lebanese belly dancers

Lebanese singer Fayrouz

the *dabke*, the Lebanese national dance. It is usually performed at a *hafla*, or dinner dance. People of all ages join in this lively folk dance, holding hands in either a circle or a line. Another form of traditional dance still seen in Lebanon is classical belly dancing. It's often performed at weddings and in nightclubs.

Lebanon's young people listen to the pop music that is enjoyed in other Arab nations as well. Since it began in Egypt in the 1970s, this musical style has evolved from something with clanky rhythms and synthesized vocals into a more fluid sound with lots of piano, guitar, and drums. Among the current favorites in Lebanon's pop music scene is The 4 Cats, an all-female band.

The most popular singer in Lebanon's history is Fayrouz. Born and raised in Beirut, she began singing professionally in the 1950s. Her fame grew throughout the 1960s and '70s, when the folklore movement in Lebanon took hold among artists of all types. Fayrouz' songs, sung in her dinstinctive velvety voice, were in touch with the emotions of many Lebanese. She gave musical voice to their hopes and dreams, their wishes for the country and for their families. She left Lebanon for Paris during the civil war but then returned to Beirut and resumed her career.

Lebanon's Museums

It's not surprising that a nation with as rich a culture and history as Lebanon would support numerous museums. Perhaps the most important is the National Museum in Beirut, which opened in 1942. Among its approximately 1,300 ancient items from throughout Lebanon are examples of early alphabetical writing, statues, mosaics, and sarcophagi, or stone coffins.

The sarcophagus of King Hiram of Byblos (below) is

considered the highlight among the many priceless pieces here. Dating back to the tenth century B.C., it is decorated with paintings of the king and a Phoenician inscription. The writings, some of the earliest examples of the Phoenician alphabet ever found, are a warning to anyone who might rob or vandalize the sarcophagus, predicting terrible things to come.

During Lebanon's civil war, museum officials went to great lengths to protect the artifacts from damage during the bombings. Some items were removed, and others were put away in the museum basement. Some of the largest, most valuable pieces were encased in plastic and cement. Unfortunately the museum still suffered a great deal of damage (above). It took several years after the war to repair the building and its displays. The museum's reopening in 1999 is a part of Lebanon's history itself.

Marriage Customs in Lebanon

Marriages in Lebanon are religious affairs, and each faith has its own customs and traditions. Religious leaders have authority to perform marriages, as well as to make decisions regarding divorce.

A Muslim wedding ceremony is called *al-kitab*, and the bride and the groom are married by a religious official in the bride's house or in a mosque. The ceremony is accompanied by great happiness and celebration. In small villages, nearly everyone participates. They help clean the house and prepare the food, and they offer gifts and good wishes. Some wealthy families celebrate for as long as thirty days, while even poor families celebrate for three days.

Christian weddings are performed by priests, usually in churches. Again, these are joyous events, and many friends and family join in the celebrations.

If a couple is not religious, or if they are from different faiths, getting married in Lebanon is a challenge. There are no nonreligious, civil ceremonies performed in Lebanon. Nearly a quarter of all Lebanese couples want a civil ceremony, but to get one they must leave the country. Most head to Cyprus.

Horseback riding is a leisurely pursuit along Lebanon's beaches.

Sports

Lebanese are social and friendly people who enjoy their leisure time. They typically participate in sporting activities that are not too competitive, such as bowling, hiking, and bicycling. Volleyball and ping-pong are popular, too.

With so many people living along the Mediterranean coast, water sports are popular. Lebanese enjoy sailing, fishing, and swimming. Scuba divers report seeing sunken boats and other objects, along with natural underwater sights.

Lebanese Football

Lebanon does not have a professional football team (soccer team to North Americans), but there are a few clubs that generate the same kind of enthusiasm among fans. One of these is Nejmeh Sporting Club, founded in Beirut in 1945 by a group of young men who just wanted to play football. It grew through the years into a team that included some of the nation's best players. The 1970s were a particularly glorious period for the team, as it dominated Lebanese football and earned respect around the world. But then the civil war began, and like many things in Lebanon at the time, Nejmeh Sporting Club suffered greatly. Sporting events were just too far from the minds of people who were trying to stay alive, and the team dwindled. But it began to rebuild soon after the war, and Nejmeh Sporting Club is once again a strong team. Though its players are not professional, they do earn an income, and many are able to hold other jobs on the side as well. The club would like to find a corporate sponsor with enough money to help it become a professional team, but in the meantime the players are content with being some of Lebanon's best and most-watched athletes.

In Lebanon's Cedars area, sports enthusiasts are able to enjoy activities that are not normally associated with the Middle East. The snow that falls at higher elevations makes it possible for them to snowboard and ski. They can even ride snowmobiles in some places.

A few spectator sports have large followings, though. Top on the list is football—the game North Americans call soccer—and the local teams have many fans. A lot of people enjoy basketball, too. Auto racing and horse racing are both popular in Beirut, where there are good facilities for people to watch both types of events.

Lebanon had only a small showing at the 2004 Summer Olympics in Athens, Greece, including one athlete who competed in the men's high jump. But the country's international sports participation will soon be expanding.

Lebanon will be hosting the 2009 Winter Asian Games, which are expected to attract some 1,800 athletes representing more than thirty Asian delegations. The games will likely give a great boost to tourism, as Lebanon's beautiful, snowy mountainous region will be publicized as the backdrop for the games. Officials are eager to increase enthusiasm for winter sports in Lebanon, especially ice hockey, ice-skating, ski jumping, curling, speed skating, and cross-country skiing. These are sports not normally associated with Middle Eastern culture, but Lebanon's diverse climate can support them.

Culture and art are an important part of Lebanese history, absorbing creative and enriching influences during the good times and soothing people's troubles during the bad times.

Life in Lebanon

Assortment of Lebanese dishes

DAILY LIFE IN LEBANON IS NOT VERY DIFFERENT FROM that in much of the rest of the world. People enjoy their families, share meals, and go to work and school. Lebanese people often manage to add their own twist to things, however, creating a distinct lifestyle.

Food

People around the world enjoy Lebanese food. There are restaurants serving Lebanese cuisine in most international cities, and recipe books featuring Lebanon's food abound. It's

Opposite: **Shoppers can buy fresh vegetables daily at the market in Beirut.**

Street Food

Eating on the street is a popular way to enjoy a quick meal or snack in Lebanon. Vendors line up on busy streets to cook their food outside and sell it to the passersby. *Falafel*, fried chickpea balls, is a popular street food, as is *fuul*, fava beans often served mashed.

Lebanese tabbouleh

a cooking style that blends traditional Middle Eastern ingredients and methods with special touches from French and Turkish cuisine. The result is delicious food, bursting with flavor and unique among cuisines.

In Lebanon, however, people don't consider their meals to be exotic, just delicious. The food is often inexpensive, making use of ingredients that are plentiful and easy to obtain and store. Spices add the special touch. The day begins with breakfast, often a pastry. Typical Lebanese pastries include *manakish*, brushed with olive oil and baked with such seasonings as thyme and sesame seeds. Another popular breakfast meal is *kishk*, a fried mixture of bulgar wheat and yogurt, flavored with garlic and onions.

The second meal of the day, usually served in the midafternoon, is also the largest. It often begins with a selection of hot and cold appetizers, called *mezze*. These can include spinach pie, dried cheese, and *pita*, a soft, flat bread. It's served with dips such as *hummus*, made with chickpeas and a sesame paste called *tahini*. Another mezze might be *tabbouleh*, a cold salad made from softened bulgar wheat, flavored with tomatoes, mint, and parsley. Other options are pizza and grape leaves stuffed with meat and rice.

Mezze is followed by the main course, usually lamb, chicken, or fish.

Meat is sometimes filled with a stuffing of nuts and rice. *Kibbeh* is a mixture of ground lamb and bulgar wheat served in several ways—raw, baked in a pie, or fried. Kebabs, or chunks of meat, are skewered on sticks. Both lamb and chicken are often served in this way. Rice or potatoes, or sometimes another serving of pita or a thin bread called *marcook*, are the accompaniment. People also enjoy fruits and vegetables along with their meals. The finishing touch is often a sweet dessert of custard or *baklava*, a syrupy pastry filled with nuts and spices.

Lebanese enjoy baklava after a meal.

Ali the Trend-Setter

Coffee is popular throughout Lebanon, without a doubt. The person credited with bringing the beverage to Lebanon is Ali, son of the Muslim religious leader Mohammed bin Iraq al-Dimashqi. Ali's family lived in Beirut until 1517, when the father left on a pilgrimage to Mecca, leaving Ali behind. Mohammed died there in 1526. Upon hearing of the death of his father, Ali was terribly upset. He took off for Mecca immediately and stayed for nearly fifteen years. During that time he developed a strong liking for the Arab custom of drinking coffee.

As he prepared to return to Beirut, he knew no one there drank coffee. But he wasn't willing to give up his habit. He brought several sacks of coffee beans back with him. When his friends tried the beverage, they enjoyed it too. The trend quickly caught on throughout the area.

The trend provided potters with a new opportunity: producing the cups used for drinking coffee. Centuries later archaeologists unearthed hundreds of small cups in areas that had been souqs. They are just one sign of how popular coffee—the drink Ali brought to Lebanon—quickly became.

The same sorts of foods are served in the evening, though dinner is a lighter meal. Most adults drink strong Turkish coffee. Popular soft drinks include *ayran*, made from yogurt, and *jellab*, made from raisins and served with pine nuts.

Family Life

Most Lebanese live in cities, often in high-rise apartment buildings. Some older neighborhoods include houses constructed of limestone, bricks, or concrete, with roofs of thatch or tile. Most villages include a souq, or outdoor market, and large cities have several souqs, along with modern shopping malls. Merchants set up small areas in the souq to sell the foods they produce or the crafts they create. It's possible to purchase traditional embroidered scarves, just-picked vegetables, handmade soap, fresh pastries, and copper pots all in one trip to a souq.

Family bonds are important to Lebanese people. Even after children are grown, get married, and have children of their own, many choose to live very near their parents and siblings. All the adults in the family cooperate in caring for the children, who often spend time with grandparents and aunts and uncles.

High-rise apartments in Beirut house many who live in the city.

Most Lebanese women stay home to take care of their families, while the men work and socialize mostly with other men. The women typically make many decisions for the family and are equal partners with their husbands. In recent years, though, the trend has been for more and more women to join the ranks of working people. Today they account for about a third of the workforce. Lebanese women work in such fields as government, medicine, engineering, law, and education.

A female news reporter prepares for a broadcast before going on the air.

Backgammon

Lebanese people enjoy a variety of games when they get together, including a type of checkers called *dama*, chess, and such card games as bridge and a Middle Eastern game called *basra*. Basra is played with two to four people, who match cards to make captures and earn points. But walk into nearly any coffeehouse or home and you are likely to find a backgammon board. Usually these are made by hand, with ornate decorations. Frequently, they are in use.

Backgammon (above) is the world's oldest-known game. It began some four thousand years ago near Lebanon, in the region that is now Syria, Iran, and Iraq. Stones were used as markers on wooden boards in the early days.

Today it is a popular game in which players move around the board according to a roll of the dice and seek to eliminate their opponent's markers. Strategy is an important part of the game, so players can continue to improve their skills and enjoy playing backgammon throughout their lives.

Education is important in Lebanon. Almost 90 percent of all Lebanese can read.

Education

Lebanese people in general are a well-educated group. Nearly 90 percent of all Lebanese are literate, or able to read. This is one of the highest literacy rates in the Middle East.

Though each student is required by law to attend only five years of primary school, most go longer, attending up to an additional seven years of secondary school. During the last three years, they can choose either a vocational direction that will lead them into the workforce when they graduate or academics leading on to college. Students attend school from 8 A.M. to 5 P.M. each day and usually have homework at night.

Public schools are free, but more than half of all parents choose to send their children to private schools. The majority of these are run by religious institutions. Lebanon has twenty-three universities and other institutions of higher learning enabling students to specialize in many fields, including education, law, science, medicine, and agriculture.

Holidays in Lebanon

Many of the holidays celebrated in Lebanon are religious events, observed only by Muslims or only by Christians. There are a few days, however, celebrated by all Lebanese people. Among these, the most important is Independence Day, on November 22. Parties are held in homes throughout the country. The festivities begin right at midnight, when car horns honk, ships' horns blare through the harbors, and bells ring out from doors and front yards everywhere in the country. The streets are filled through the day with people joyfully marking this important day.

New Year's Day	January 1
Feast of Saint Maron	February 9
May Day	May 1
Labor Day	May 1
Martyrs' Day	May 6
All Saints' Day	November 1
Independence Day	November 22
Christmas	December 25
Easter	March or April
Ras as-Sana, or New Year's Day	First day of the Islamic calendar
Ramadan	Ninth month of the Islamic calendar
Eid al-Fitr	End of Ramadan
Eid al-Adha	10th–13th of the twelfth month of the Islamic calendar

Lebanon has a reputation throughout the Middle East for having excellent health care. There are about 150 hospitals in Lebanon, most of which are privately run. Wealthy people are

Health care is a priority for all in Lebanon.

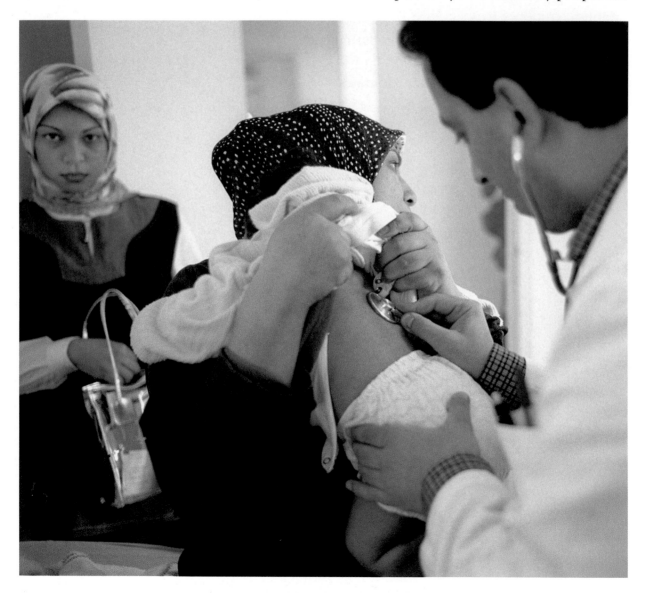

able to afford the best medical treatment, but only the very poor people living in the country's most remote areas are unable to get at least basic care.

In urban areas it is quite easy to get medical care. Doctors have a special symbol on their car so that when they're driving, people in emergencies can flag them down immediately. Medicines are readily available in pharmacies, and a national medical insurance plan helps cover costs.

Some medical experts feel that the biggest health problem in Lebanon today may be the stress that still lingers in people following the years of devastating civil war. Though Lebanese people are quite willing to seek medical care, they are hesitant to seek help for psychological and emotional problems. There is a tendency in the culture to feel that these types of issues should be dealt with privately or in the family. They refuse to seek professional help and therefore end up living with a lot of stress. Sometimes too much pent-up stress can lead to physical problems, though, and doctors are seeing the result of this in Lebanon. People are suffering from such ailments as heart disease, headaches, and stomach problems.

Lingering issues from Lebanon's civil war continue to cause some problems for its citizens. The end of the war also brought with it challenges—challenges in government, in the environment, and in society and religion. But Lebanese people are working hard to bring their country back from the low point of war. They are meeting many of these challenges and taking the country to new heights.

Timeline

Lebanese History		World History
People begin to settle on Lebanon's shores.	**10,000** B.C.	
Coastal cities form into Phoenicia.	**3000** B.C.	
	2500 B.C.	Egyptians build the Pyramids and the Sphinx in Giza.
Assyrians, Babylonians, and Persians conquer Phoenicia.	**867–538** B.C.	**563** B.C. The Buddha is born in India.
Greeks conquer much of the Middle East, including land that is now Lebanon.	**Fourth century** B.C.	
Christianity has its beginnings in Lebanon and neighboring areas.	**First century** A.D.	
The Roman army takes over, and Phoenicia becomes part of the Byzantine Empire.	**64**	
	A.D. **313**	The Roman emperor Constantine recognizes Christianity.
Islam becomes popular in Lebanon.	**636**	**610** The Prophet Muhammad begins preaching a new religion called Islam.
	1054	The Eastern (Orthodox) and Western (Roman) Churches break apart.
	1066	William the Conqueror defeats the English in the Battle of Hastings.
The Crusades begin; Christians occupy Lebanon and surrounding areas.	**1095**	**1095** Pope Urban II proclaims the First Crusade.
Crusaders are forced out of Lebanon and elsewhere. The Crusades end.	**1291**	**1215** King John seals the Magna Carta.
	1300s	The Renaissance begins in Italy.
	1347	The Black Death sweeps through Europe.
	1453	Ottoman Turks capture Constantinople, conquering the Byzantine Empire.
	1492	Columbus arrives in North America.
Lebanon becomes part of the Ottoman Empire.	**1516**	**1500s** The Reformation leads to the birth of Protestantism.
	1776	The Declaration of Independence is signed.
Beirut becomes a major port for trade in Middle East.	**1840**	**1789** The French Revolution begins.
Lebanon is divided in two, led by Christians in the north and Druze in the south. Fighting erupts.	**1842**	

Lebanese History

The Ottoman foreign minister attempts to end warfare.	1860
Peace treaties end fighting in Lebanon.	1867
Lebanon becomes a mandate of France.	1920
The Lebanese constitution is approved.	1926
Lebanon becomes an independent nation.	1943
Refugees enter Lebanon following the Suez crisis.	1956
American troops restore order after Lebanese Muslims oppose President Camille Chamoun.	1958
Israel bombs Lebanon after an Israeli airplane is attacked by Arab terrorists claiming to be from a Palestinian refugee camp in Lebanon.	1968
Israel attacks Lebanon following attacks on Israel's Tel Aviv airport and Israeli athletes during the Summer Olympics.	1972
Lebanon's civil war begins.	1975
Fighting flares up again between Christian and Syrian militias.	1978
A cease-fire agreement is signed, but the war does not end.	1981
Israel invades Lebanon.	1982
Israeli forces leave most of Lebanon, but fighting continues.	1985
Lebanon's civil war ends. Years of rebuilding Lebanon begin.	1991
Israel withdraws from the south Lebanon "security zone."	1999
Israel continues occasional attacks on southern Lebanon.	2003

World History

1865	The American Civil War ends.
1914	World War I breaks out.
1917	The Bolshevik Revolution brings communism to Russia.
1929	Worldwide economic depression begins.
1939	World War II begins, following the German invasion of Poland.
1945	World War II ends.
1957	The Vietnam War starts.
1969	Humans land on the moon.
1975	The Vietnam War ends.
1979	Soviet Union invades Afghanistan.
1983	Drought and famine in Africa.
1989	The Berlin Wall is torn down, as communism crumbles in Eastern Europe.
1991	Soviet Union breaks into separate states.
1992	Bill Clinton is elected U.S. president.
2000	George W. Bush is elected U.S. president.
2001	Terrorists attack World Trade Towers, New York and the Pentagon, Washington, D.C.
2003	A coalition of forty-nine nations, headed by the United States and Great Britain, invade Iraq.

Fast Facts

Official name: al-Jumhuriyah al-Lubananiyah,
                     Republic of Lebanon

Capital: Beirut

Official language: Arabic

Beirut

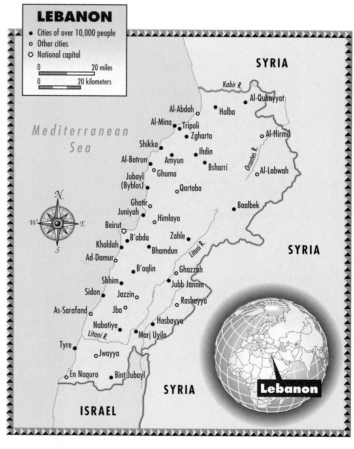

Lebanon's flag

Lebanese mountains

Official religion:	None
Year of founding:	1943
National anthem:	"Kulluna lil watan lil'ula lil'alam" ("All of Us for Our Country, Glory, Flag")
Government:	Constitutional republic
Head of government:	Prime minister
Head of state:	President
Area of country:	4,015 square miles (10,399 sq km)
Greatest distance north to south:	120 miles (190 km)
Greatest distance east to west:	50 miles (80 km)
Land and water borders:	Syria to the north and east, Israel to the south, and the Mediterranean Sea to the west.
Highest elevation:	10,131 feet (3,088 m) at Qurnet as Sawda
Lowest elevation:	Sea level at the Mediterranean Sea coastline
Highest average temperature:	90°F (32°C)
Lowest average temperature:	55°F (13°C)
Average annual precipitation:	Coast, 35 inches (89 cm); mountains, 50 inches (127 cm)

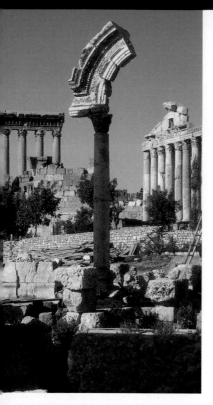

Baalbek

National population: 3,727,703 (2003 est.)

Population of largest cities (2003 est):

Beirut	1,171,000
Tripoli	212,900
Sidon	149,000
Tyre	117,100
Nabatiye	89,400

Famous landmarks:
- ▶ *Pigeon Rocks*, Beirut
- ▶ *Temple of Jupiter*, Baalbek
- ▶ *Sea Castle*, Sidon
- ▶ *National Museum*, Beirut
- ▶ *Qurnet as Sawda*, southeast of Tripoli
- ▶ *Roman Hippodrome*, Tyre
- ▶ *The Citadel of Raymond de Saint-Gilles*, Tripoli

Industry: Products manufactured include clothing, processed food, and jewelry for the retail market, as well as pharmaceuticals, aluminum, textiles, and cement. Among the products mined are salt, gypsum, tin, lignite, iron ore, and limestone. The major agriculture products are grapes, potatoes, tomatoes, cucumbers, apples, citrus, olives, and tobacco.

Currency: The Lebanese pound. One pound = 100 paisters. As of September 2004, 1,514.00 Lebanese pounds equaled U.S. $1

System of weights and measures: metric system

Literacy rate: 90 percent

Lebanese currency

Schoolgirl

Khalil Gibran

Common Arabic Words and Phrases:

as-salamu :alai-kum	hello (Literally,: "Peace be with you")
wa :alai-kum as-salaam	reply to hello
al-Hamdu li-l-aáah	Praise be to God
sabaah al-khair	good morning
sabaah an-nuur	reply to good morning
masa' al-khair	good evening
masaa an-nuur	reply to good evening
shukran	thank you
asif	I am sorry

Famous Lebanese:

Saint Aquilina *Catholic martyr*	(281–293)
Saint Charbel *Catholic monk*	(1828–1898)
Fakhr al-Din M'an *Founder of modern Lebanon*	(1570–1635)
Fayrouz *Singer*	(1935–)
Khalil Gibran *Writer and artist*	(1883–1931)
al Hakim bin Amrillah *Divine leader of Druze*	(996–1021)
Rafiq Hariri *Lebanese prime minister*	(1944–)
King Hiram *Ruler*	(989–936 B.C.)
Amin Maalouf *Writer*	(1949–)
Emily Nasrallah *Writer*	(1931–)
Saint Rafka *Catholic nun*	(1832–1914)
Hanan Al-Shaykh *Writer*	(1945–)

To Find Out More

Nonfiction

▶ Grolier Educational Staff. *Fiesta! Lebanon*. Danbury, CT: Grolier, 1999.

▶ Hutchinson, Linda. *Lebanon*. San Diego: Lucent, 2003.

▶ Jenkins, Siona, and Ann Jousiffe. *Lebanon*. Melbourne, Australia: Lonely Planet Publications, 2001.

▶ McDaniel, Jan, ed. Foreign Policy Research Institute. *Lebanon*. Broomall, PA: Mason Crest Publishers, 2003.

▶ Skahill, Carolyn. *A Historical Atlas of Lebanon*. New York: Rosen Publishing Group, 2003.

Web sites

▶ **Lebanon Panorama**
www.lebanonpanorama.com
Historical and cultural information combined with beautiful panoramic images.

▶ **Lebanon Cultural Profiles Project**
www.settlement.org/cp/english/lebanon/index.html
Cultural Profiles Project, with information on Lebanon's geography, family life, sports, food, education, holidays, and more.

▶ **Lebanon Links**
http://almashriq.hiof.no/lebanon
Links to many Lebanese topics.

▶ **Embassy of Lebanon**
www.lebanonembassyus.org
*Published by the Lebanese Embassy,
the site contains information on the
country's history, government, economy, and culture, as well as a "Kids
Only" section.*

Embassies

▶ **Lebanese Embassy in the
United States**
2560 28th St. NW
Washington, DC 20008
(202) 939-6300

▶ **Lebanese Embassy in Canada**
640 Lyon St.
Ottawa, Ontario K15 3ZS
(613) 236-5825

Index

Page numbers in *italics* indicate illustrations.

Meet the Author

Whenever Terri Willis begins researching a topic for a book, it feels like the start of a journey.

"I spend so much time reading and thinking about the countries as I write about them, I sometimes feel like I'm there," she said.

The journey begins at the local library, where Terri checks out all the materials she can find on a country—books, magazines, videos. She spends several days poring over all the information, to get a feel for where she'll be going with the book.

Bookstores often provide more materials. Good travel guides can be very helpful. For her book on Lebanon, Terri particularly enjoyed the *Lonely Planet* guide to Lebanon. It contains beautiful photography and a lot of great information about the nation and its people.

Then Terri heads to Memorial Library at the University of Wisconsin-Madison. "It's always fun to go back to the campus where I earned my degree," she said. "The library there is full of treasures."

The Internet is another good source for material. It's important to use only reliable sources though. Anybody can create a Web site and put anything on it, so not all Internet content is credible. Terri is careful to use only information that comes from places such as universities and government agencies. Even then it's good to remember that some of these sources may not present the whole picture. A thorough search is important.

Terri fills out her research by talking to people and asking questions. Embassies, chambers of commerce, government agencies, universities—all have knowledgeable people who are willing to help.

Terri has a degree in journalism. Her books include *Libya, Romania, Vietnam, Venezuela, Democratic Republic of the Congo,* and *Qatar* in the Enchantment of the World series. Other books for Children's Press include *Land Use and Abuse, Cars: an Environmental Challenge* (coauthored by Wallace B. Black), and *Restoring Nature: Land*.

Terri lives in Cedarburg, Wisconsin, where she is an educator in the public schools and a Girl Scout leader. She shares her home with her husband, Harry, and their two daughters, Andrea and Elizabeth.

Photo Credits

Photographs © 2005:

AP/Wide World Photos: 86 (EPA), 64, 80 (Hussein Malla), 67 (Saleh Rifai), 122 (Norbert Schiller/EPA), 73

Aurora: 96 (Peter Essick), 126 (Frederic Noy/Cosmos)

Bridgeman Art Library International Ltd., London/New York: 41 (Guildhall Library, Corporation of London, UK)

Brown Brothers: 43

Bruce Coleman Inc./Mark Newman: 33 bottom

Corbis Images: cover, 6, 106 (Paul Almasy), 7 bottom, 42 (Archivo Iconofrafico, SA), 55, 56, 93, 108, 133 bottom (Bettmann), 46 (Christie's Images), 118 (Conde Nast Archive), 111 bottom (Gianni Dagli Orti), 11 Francoise de Mulder), 104 top (Grzegorz Galazka), 53, 57 (Hulton-Deutsch Collection), 31 top (Jacqui Hurst), 74, 90, 98, 100, 112, 113 (Ed Kashi), 61 (Alain Keler), 32 bottom (Layne Kennedy), 34 (Samer Mohdad), 111 top (Christine Osborne), 121 (Carmen Redondo), 59, 60 bottom (Reza/Webistan), 2 (Jamal Saidi/Reuters), 37 (Kevin Schafer), 44 bottom (Stapleton Collection), 124, 133 top (David Turnley), 8, 14, 17, 21, 23, 71 bottom, 88, 116 (Roger Wood), 71 top, 130 left (Alison Wright)

Corbis Sygma: 109 top (Sophie Bassouls), 87 (Bernard Bisson), 110 bottom (Jacques Langevin), 35 (Attar Maher)

Dembinsky Photo Assoc./Mary Clay: 31 bottom

Getty Images: 77 (AFP), 65 (Joseph Barrak/AFP), 68 (Ramzi Haidar/AFP), 60 top (Keystone), 62, 92 (Suhaila Sahmarani/AFP)

Hulton | Archive/Getty Images: 30 top

Landov, LLC/Fadi Asaad/Reuters: 114

Larry Luxner: 9, 16

North Wind Picture Archives: 48

Peter Arnold Inc./Wolfgang Kunz/ Bilderberg: 82

Photri Inc.: 20 left, 20 right, 83 bottom

PictureQuest/Bob Dammrich/Stock Boston Inc.: 110 top

Robertstock.com/K. Sholz: 24, 132 top

Superstock, Inc.: 32 top (Tom Brakefield), 33 top (James Urbach), 18

TRIP Photo Library: 7 top, 19, 26, 27, 28, 29, 30 bottom, 39, 40, 75, 76, 85, 101, 102, 104 bottom, 109 bottom, 119, 131 bottom, 132 bottom (Helene Rogers), 49, 51, 97, 99, 123

Viesti Collection, Inc./Helene Rogers: 89, 117

Woodfin Camp & Associates: 34 bottom (R. Frerck), 12 (Barry Iverson)

Maps by XNR Productions Inc.